The Rose Metal Press Field Guide to Writing

FLASH FICTION

D1375424

Advance Praise for
The Rose Metal Press Field Guide to Writing Flash Fiction

"*The Field Guide to Flash Fiction* is an exhaustive, thoughtful, idea-producing guide to one of the lesser-known forms of literary expression, the short short story—I can't imagine that there's anything left out of this remarkable anthology of essays about flash fiction. It should prompt the neophyte and the veteran writer to get busy and try one of these difficult stories."

—Anne Bernays,
coauthor of *What If? Writing Exercises for Fiction Writers*

"As professors of English, we find *The Field Guide* invaluable. The essays are cogent, clear, and short—to the point. Students wishing to practice creative fiction are provided with tools, theory, and inspiration throughout each step of the composition process. Writers reading about literature and then reading the literature itself will discover how effectively *The Field Guide* presents concepts as it eschews academic jargon in favor of a hands-on approach."

—Jon Redfern and Jack David,
editors of *Short Short Stories*

"How many words does it take to tell an important story? In the many words contained in *The Field Guide*, written by masters of the short-short fiction form, you may begin to understand. Or not. There always remains the mystery that is fiction itself. Let's be glad."

—James Thomas,
co-editor of *Sudden Fiction* and *Flash Fiction Forward*

Field Guide to Writing

Flash
Fiction

Tips from Editors, Teachers, and Writers in the Field

Edited by Tara L. Masih

Rose Metal Press

2009

Acknowledgments for previously published works appear on page 164, which constitutes an extension of the copyright page.

Rose Metal Press, Inc.
P.O. Box 1956
Brookline, MA 02446
rosemetalpress@gmail.com
www.rosemetalpress.com

Library of Congress Control Number: 2009903584

ISBN: 978-0-9789848-6-1

Cover and interior design by Rebecca Saraceno
Cover typefaces: Avenir and Utopia; Interior typefaces: Utopia, with Avenir
See "A Note About the Type" for more information about the type.

This book is manufactured in the United States of America and printed on acid-free paper.

This book is partially sponsored by a grant from the Massachusetts Cultural Council.

massculturalcouncil.org

TABLE OF CONTENTS

SURVEYING THE LANDSCAPE
A Preface

Back in November of 2007, Tara L. Masih sent us an email that began, "I just had this idea this morning and did some quick research."

Intrigued, we read on and learned that it had occurred to Tara that there were virtually no books devoted solely to the study, writing, and practice of flash fiction. The letter was a pitch, of course, and she wanted us to consider publishing such a book. Tara, with her skills as an editor and her many years of textbook publishing experience, would serve as editor in chief.

Although our press had only been in existence for two years at that point, short short fiction had already become a flagship genre of ours, so it was natural that Tara should think of us as a possible prospect. Perversely, though, it was our fondness for flash fiction itself that caused our initial interest in her idea to be mixed with skepticism and resistance.

Because while Rose Metal Press is enamored of hybrid genres and forms and seeks to give them a forum for publication, we do not want to pin said inventive forms down with strict definitions, nor do we want to sink their ever-changing manifestations beneath the weight of scholarly scrutiny and analysis.

Fortunately, neither did Tara.

Her vision for the project—the angle of approach that won us over—was that it should avoid dryness and technicality. Instead of setting parameters or rules, the book should be brief and accessible, a book of ideas about and for flash fiction; it should be creative and capable of being read just for pleasure, as well as used as a teaching tool; and its very brevity and tone should reflect the art of the flash fiction story.

Her plan to gather personal essays on the craft of flash fiction from respected and innovative editors, teachers, and writers of the form under the cover of one book made perfect sense. In this way, the book would not attempt to be "definitive" or "exhaustive," but could instead be used, as Tara's proposed title suggested, as a *Field Guide*. Each quick essay would be followed by an exercise or prompt as well as an example designed to illustrate, not unlike the color plates of an Audubon or Peterson guide, the concept in question.

"I love the idea of calling it a *field guide*," Tara wrote in her proposal. "The phrase for me signifies a less formal creative manual of brief, spontaneous observations." We loved it, too.

The *Field Guide* that follows is the realization of Tara's timely proposal to highlight a beloved genre that has been somewhat marginalized by lack of published discussion of the form itself and its mechanisms. Flash fiction is burgeoning, with significant growth in the number of people writing and publishing short shorts. This flourishing is due in part to a strong online presence and a proliferation of journals dedicated to the form, and especially to the number of college- and graduate-level workshops dedicated to the writing of flash. Our hope is that bringing together this collection of essays on flash that is neither purely academic nor purely anecdotal will provide a resource for the reader, student, writer, or teacher of flash fiction—really, for all of the above.

Tara's **introduction** offers, for the first time, an in-depth history of flash fiction, following the genre through its hitherto virtually unknown early publications and appearances, to periods of renaissance and hibernation, to the coining of the name flash fiction, to its current state and practice.

Twenty-five conversational, reflective essays follow the introduction, each one illuminating a different idea about editing, teaching, or writing flash. The table of contents groups the essays by theme, which helps direct readers and teachers to subjects of particular interest. Each essay ends with an **exercise** or **prompt**, as well as a **story example** so that readers can directly apply the musings of the essayist to their own writing or study. These diverse and talented essayists range from the pioneers of the contemporary field, to well-known teachers of flash, to editors of flash-focused publications, to new innovators in the genre.

The *Field Guide* closes with a list of **further readings** suggested by the essayists, the editor, and the press that we hope will showcase the richness of the field and offer suggestions to readers, teachers, and students alike.

It's not necessarily the case that you will be able, even hiking the whole path of this book, to see all the flora and fauna this particular "field" has to offer. But you will see a lot, and what you see will give you a personal impression and a well-rounded look at the weird and wonderful hybrid species that populate the landscape of flash fiction. Hopefully, you'll make your own notes of discovery in the margins.

–Abigail Beckel & Kathleen Rooney

Rose Metal Press
Boston, MA, 2009

IN PURSUIT OF THE SHORT SHORT STORY
An Introduction

"Each drop encases its own separate note, the way each drop engulfs its own blue pearl of light." This description of rain, from Stuart Dybek's story "Nighthawks," is as close to a definition of flash fiction as I can personally offer. A successful flash enchants us, each small story successfully rendered engulfing us for a brief moment—in a "flash," as many of the writers within suggest—in its own brand of light, or truth. And the effects linger on, sometimes for decades.

To offer a more complete, hard-edged definition is virtually impossible. Outside of a page or word count (roughly 1–3 pages and 250–1,000 words), the definitions offered by experts can leave a writer unsure of how to characterize flash. To say that a flash must contain all the literary elements that a longer story does—plot, setting, character, conflict, narration—would be argued against by the proponents of experimental flash who lean more toward slice-of-life sketches. In the end, a flash is simply a story in miniature, a work of art carved on a grain of rice—something of import to the artist or writer that is confined and reduced, either by design or outcome, into a small square space using the structural devices of prose line and paragraph form with the purpose of creating an intense, emotional impact.

It can't be denied that flash fiction, or what was originally known as (and is still often called) the short short story, is having a revival after several decades of losing its audience. The growth of MFA writing programs in the 1980s, which in turn stimulated the growth of literary magazines as necessary forums for the placement of protégés' work, brought these brief experiments in prose to the attention of Robert Shapard (p. 87) and James Thomas. Editors of the highly acclaimed

Sudden Fiction and *Flash Fiction* anthologies, they set off an unexpected wave of interest in the short short story that has reached most continents. Fueled by Internet magazines that often seek short shorts for easy viewing to please an audience growing increasingly intolerant of lengthy blocks of text, short prose is sure to remain popular, at least until the next great technological advancement forces another major lifestyle change.

When I began writing this historical introduction, I was intent on finding the first time the phrase *short short story* was formally used. Just how old was this genre? I expected to go no further back than perhaps the 1950s to find the phrase, and certainly no further back than Hemingway's *In Our Time* for an example of such works. Yet I was surprised and soon overwhelmed by the broad history and wealth of intercultural influences and examples.

Why this surprise? Because as a former English literature major and an editor of countless English literature texts, I have learned that many American critics and scholars hold dearly to the belief that the short story is distinctly an American invention. But they are beginning to explore the fact that, while U.S. story writers such as Washington Irving and Nathaniel Hawthorne *were* instrumental in honing down the epic novels of the early nineteenth century, writers on other shores were developing their own distinctive prose and poetic styles, which returned back to our shores to further impact us.

I was excited to discover that the short short story has its own path of development. It didn't take an abrupt turn away from its heftier cousin the short story; it evolved casually alongside it until it found its place in nineteenth-century periodicals, during a time when literature was no longer being written solely for the upper class.

But prior to exploring the short short story's history, it's important to touch on what makes stories necessary to all cultures, as this necessity is the impetus behind the short short's evolution. Because before recorded stories, and the stories that make up the major religious works, before even the fireside stories and the lyrical stories sung by wandering minstrels, there was the chant, the root of all storytelling—first person, rhythmic, repetitive. Chants were necessary retellings of events meant to record tribal history and to raise the individual to some level above that of the ordinary.

Telling stories, it seems, is natural to all societies and appears to play a part in our individual and communal health. As Carl Jung, believer in the collective unconscious, writes, "Pathology comes from a story untold." Childhood development can be traced from focus on the self toward an increasing focus on others, and our ancestors' stories evolved in a similar manner, from early first-person survival stories to more universal third-person mysteries—thus, the birth of myth and folk tales.

From there, the oral tradition gradually moved to the written in Europe. In Italy in the 1300s Giovanni Boccaccio (1313–75) found fame with his novella *The Decameron*, a collection of short prose stories narrated by young women and men who escaped the Black Death. Italy continued to have a strong influence on European writers, including William Shakespeare (1564–1616), who relied heavily on Italian writers as a source for his plots. Some believe his story poems written in 1592–94 are also an early inspiration to the development of the short story.

Meanwhile in Asia, artists were telling stories in pictures: miniatures in India, and ukiyo-e (or "pictures of the floating world") in Japan. The Japanese pictures depicted scenes of what was becoming a progressively more urban world from the start of the 1600s into the 1800s. The illustrations incorporated literary and historical allusions and symbols, stories within stories. Often, the images were accompanied by written text. Just as periodicals began to rise in number and popularity in the West, devoured by an ever more literate populace, these illustrations became so sought after by Japan's merchant class that the illustrated books could no longer be produced and sewn by hand; the demand was too high. Ukiyo-e thus became the first illustrated books printed using wood blocks, accessible even to the illiterate because they could "read" the pictures.

These gradual movements toward written, realistic short prose and stories for the masses would provide something that audiences craved, immersing them in universal truths to which they could relate, taking them beyond religious texts and revealing another way to understand the human condition.

In his own introduction to a collection of short shorts, editor Irving Howe asks, "what could be more absurd than a long long introduction to a book of short shorts?" (xv). I could not do this history justice and set the stage for the essays and stories that follow, however, without going into that history in some length. I've done my best to be inclusive, but there are gaps, and there are writers left undiscussed who should be further explored. But that would lead to a book in itself. My hope is that others will draw from this *Field Guide* history and be inspired to fill in those gaps, or examine in more depth some of the literary icons discussed in reference to their short short works.

A History of the Short Short Story

Washington Irving and Edgar Allan Poe:
The Birth of the Western Short Story

Some literary historians believe the birth of the short story occurred with Edgar Allan Poe's 1842 critique of Nathaniel Hawthorne's collection *Twice-Told Tales*. In actual fact, the first popular American story collection was Washington Irving's *The Sketch-Book of Geoffrey Crayon, Gent.*, published in 1820 under his pseudonym at the time. This collection of observational essays, entertaining stories, and yarns brought Irving (1783–1859) acclaim on both sides of the Atlantic. *The Sketch-Book*, which had its roots in German folklore, began a trend toward shorter pieces of fiction (known as "tales," "stories," or "sketches"), and some critics feel "Rip Van Winkle," a dream story in which a "simple, good-natured" farmer lives 20 years in one night, is the true predecessor of the short short and does what minimal stories often attempt, to condense time. And like the Japanese wood-block prints that were depicting contemporary life, Irving also focused on slice-of-life stories about average people. In his own words, he was fond of "observing strange characters and manners" and, to his parents' alarm, "knew every spot where a murder or robbery had been committed, or a ghost seen" (Irving 1). Irving thus began steering American fiction away from upper-class concerns and morality issues (also known as "silver-fork fiction") and heralded the growing trend toward realism.

When Irving began writing his *Sketch-Book*, he was not in the United

States but in England. This appears to be a common theme among many of the writers of short stories that break with tradition. The authors were not only in tune with the literary works of other cultures—Henry Wadsworth Longfellow and Charles Dickens were said to have been some of Irving's influences—but were often immersed themselves, for a time, in those other cultures they admired. And as the times demanded, before appearing in book form, Irving's stories were published serially in periodicals. It is this serialization and the rise of print journalism that soon made literature a commodity.

The generous payment that periodicals could offer at that time gave Edgar Allan Poe (1809–49) the necessary means in the early 1830s to sustain himself on his short stories as he gradually became one of America's most important writers. In so doing, Poe provided the foundations for modern horror, mystery, and science fiction stories. And it was Poe who provided the context for the rules of story-building in that oft-quoted 1842 critique in *Graham's* magazine—that it be absorbed in one sitting, "with such care and skill, a picture is at length painted which leaves in the mind of him who contemplates it with a kindred art, a sense of the fullest satisfaction." Poe's own stories broke with the convention of seeking story through plot or character. Instead, he sought to capture a mood or feeling, and then to translate that same mood or feeling to the reader.

Other writers counted among the harbingers of the short short story are French writers Guy de Maupassant, whose "The Necklace" is often cited as an example of an early short short, and Colette; Russian writer Anton Chekhov; British writer Rudyard Kipling; German writer Peter Altenberg; and Franz Kafka, a Czech-born writer who wrote in German. All these writers experimented with the short story form, as did French symbolist Charles Baudelaire. In 1869, Baudelaire, a popular translator of Edgar Allan Poe, published his own *Little Prose Poems* (or *Paris Spleen*, as it is alternately titled). It contained 50 poems that explored the everyday life of lonely Parisians and is considered not only the precursor to prose poetry but to the short short story as well.

In the meantime, in America, the middle and lower classes were becoming more literate, a result of the Industrial Revolution, during which electricity and the movement from rural to urban jobs shortened the work day and lengthened the leisure hours, leaving more time to read for pleasure. Urban jobs also demanded more literacy than did farm jobs. According to the texts of the time (see the discussion on p. XXVI under "Everybody Seems to be Writing This Sort of Yarn"), the American attention span was already beginning to shrink with the advent of huge leaps forward in aviation, transportation, radio, photography, and the general quality of life. In addition, after the U.S. Civil War, when print advertising took hold and provided a means for magazines to sustain themselves, and the government dropped postal fees for mailing issues, subscription prices were lowered to a point where mass audiences could afford them. In turn, the editors had to entertain the masses and fit prose works between the lucrative, eye-catching advertisements; periodicals thus began to narrow their definition of the short story, which grew shorter.

Louisa May Alcott and Kate Chopin: The First Glimpses of Feminism in the Short Short

One lesser-known example of the early short short was penned by a Massachusetts author who took great advantage of the financial and literary opportunities afforded her by periodicals: Louisa May Alcott (1832–88) anonymously wrote many sensational, melodramatic stories, the kind which audiences demanded. However, one piece was shorter than the rest—her 3-page manifesto "Happy Women," which appeared in the *New York Ledger* in 1868 and has been categorized as a short story, a fictional essay, and a sketch, took a more serious tone. As with Irving's tales, this piece—featuring Alcott's criticism of the taboo subject of hasty matrimony and its unpleasant results for women—shows the continuing trend toward realism in American writing.

Another writer to confront feminist issues realistically was Kate Chopin (1850–1904), of Irish and French descent. As one of the United States' first bicultural story writers who spoke both English and French fluently, it's no surprise that she would greatly admire French writer Guy de Maupassant. She read his stories in the decade before she began to experiment with the genre herself in the 1890s. Of Maupassant, she states: "Here was life, not fiction; for where were the plots, the old fashioned mechanism and stage trapping . . . I had fancied were essential to

the art of story making. Here was a man [who] told us what he saw...."
(Marquand, par. 3).

By the late 1890s the public was very familiar with her work, as she appeared in many top magazines and in newspaper syndication. Her subject matter was considered controversial at the time because of her attempt to convey to readers what she saw in women's lives in the Southern Bayou, a microcosm of the greater nation. Some of her stories were very short ("The Kiss" is 1,028 words), with "The Story of an Hour" (1,007 words) being her most famous and heavily anthologized. Originally, it appeared as "The Dream of an Hour" in *Vogue* (Dec. 6, 1894), and it survives in part because of its powerful closing and surprise ending, a feature she had admired in Maupassant's work and perhaps in the work of another contemporary writer of hers, Ambrose Bierce (discussed below). In the 1970s, this 2-page story was anthologized as one of "feminism's sacred texts" by critic and editor Susan Cahill in *Women & Fiction*. That such a small work could have such an impact on generations of women proves that the power of a story does not lie in its length.

August Strindberg: The First Published Short Short Story

The earliest published example of a story I could find that strives to compress time in the manner of many modern short shorts is by Swedish writer August Strindberg (1849–1912). Famous for his plays, Strindberg also wrote and published short stories, enough to be collected into a 1903 edition titled *Sagor*, which was translated into English in 1912. In it, the story "Half a Sheet of Foolscap" ("foolscap" is sometimes translated as "paper") is less than 3 pages. Yet it manages to tell the story of a young man who has just seen off "the last moving van." A mourning-band around his arm is another early clue to the reader, as the man discovers a small sheet of foolscap tacked up on the wall near the telephone. It is a list, handwritten by his wife—"a bit of human history on half a sheet of foolscap." Along with the husband, we read through the entries of one or two words until he reaches the last entry, which in his own "plain, black letters," records the words "*The undertaker.*" Strindberg writes, "In two minutes he had relived two years of his life." And we relive it as well, the time gaps in the list taking on huge proportions.

In addition to writing, Strindberg was fascinated by and experimented with photography. He believed he could photograph "the soul," and sought to obtain psychological portraits of his subjects. He practiced pinhole photography, which further zeroes in on one small point of vision—much like a short short. I believe he may be the first writer to work to shape more into less, to focus in on that small vision in a short story. While Alcott, Chopin, and Maupassant were writing shorter works, their stories don't hinge on their briefness, but on the larger messages within their plots. Strindberg's obvious attempt to capture a marriage "in two minutes" is the heart, or soul, of his story. The details are incidental to this one literary effect.

Ambrose Bierce: Short Story Pioneer

Strindberg's plot might sound reminiscent of another short story often singled out as an early short short, not so much because of its length (3,804 words), but because of its structure and condensation of time. Like "Rip Van Winkle" and "Half a Sheet of Foolscap," "An Occurrence at Owl Creek Bridge" (1890) condenses a lengthy period of time into a small space. The author, American Ambrose Bierce (1842–1914?), known for his realism and economical style, divides his story into three parts, allowing—and some might accuse him of deliberately disorienting—the reader to think that a man about to be hung has escaped to find his way home to his wife. The reader is informed in the last two sentences that the "escape" was entirely a projection of the doomed man's unconscious, a sophisticated plot for that time period.

As with Hemingway, a later war veteran, Bierce's Civil War experiences provided him with the material and impetus for his departure from formulaic periodical plots, which still promoted linear chronology and melodramatic storylines and language, and required that the main character triumph morally in some way. Bierce's skill in poetry gave a different shape to his prose, which readers had not previously seen. Bierce's prolific career, during which he published almost 200 short stories, had a heavy influence on the horror story and on today's stories that have a dreamlike quality. This influence is far-ranging, and the impact in particular of "An Occurrence at Owl Creek Bridge" is still being felt in modern literature—the collection *Severance*, by Robert Olen Butler (p. 102), is one recent example—

and in pop culture—the ABC TV show *Lost* flashed a copy of it in book form in 2006. This story remains one of the most widely anthologized short stories of our time, even inspiring a *Twilight Zone* episode.

O. Henry: City Pictures

Bierce's success with the element of surprise set off a small literary movement. But no discussion of the short short story in the nineteenth century can be complete without mentioning William Sidney Porter, or O. Henry (1862–1910), as he is more commonly known. Convicted of embezzling from the First National Bank in Austin, Texas, he served three years in prison from 1898 to 1901. During his incarceration, he wrote stories as a means to support his daughter. Set in the Southwest and in Central America, where he had spent time avoiding extradition, these stories soon adopted that surprise twist ending he had seen being used by a writer he greatly admired, Bierce. But O. Henry's more calculated endings were of even greater consequence to the popular short short.

Continuing the trend toward stories that resonated with the more literate public, after O. Henry was released from his Ohio prison, he moved to New York, where his later writing mainly was set. His characters were ordinary urbanites. From 1903 to 1906, he published a weekly story in *New York World*, in addition to other periodicals, amassing to over 600 stories in his lifetime.

His most well-known shorts, "The Gift of the Magi" (1,800 words) and "The Last Leaf" (about 2,400 words), fall close to today's definition of flash fiction, if judged by length. If judged by plot, character, and narration, they begin to meet the standards of the flash story as well. But the most important fact is that the public loved his work, and countless fledgling writers (and some accomplished writers such as Leonard Merrick) sought to emulate it. Critic Philip Stevick writes in *The American Short Story*: "by early century there were a score of guides advising . . . ways in which the form and success of O. Henry could be duplicated" (25).

Sherwood Anderson: Country Pictures

Developing parallel to O. Henry was Sherwood Anderson (1876–1941), whose major work, a collection of stories titled *Winesburg, Ohio*, came out in 1919 when he was 40. These small-town stories deftly steered the shift even further toward writing that was growing more real and "dirty," but poetic and with psychological insight. While it preceded Kawabata's work (see p. XXI), "Paper Pills" reads like a palm-of-the-hand story. At 3 pages, it manages to explore the complete history of an unlikely marriage in a small town. And while, like his contemporary, he also seems to use not so much a twist at the end but a twist tie, the minimalist prose, exact attention to physical detail using poetic language, and the exploration of sexuality were ahead of his time and a breakaway from the more mainstream O. Henry style that could be read by the entire family.

This departure was deliberate. A follower of the impressionist movement, he believed in capturing Americans as they spoke, in their own "daily speech," and railed against the "plot short stories of the magazines—those bastard children of De Maupassant, Poe and O. Henry—it was certain there were no plot stories ever lived in any life I had known anything about" (Stevick 15). In terms of the briefness of some of his stories, he intuited that "life is but a history of moments" (Stevick 62).

Asia's Impact on the Short Short Story

Rabindranath Tagore: The First Bengali Short Story Writer

In India, Rabindranath Tagore (1861–1941) is credited with being the first Bengali short story writer. Also a painter, Tagore's prolific writing career, which emphasized poetic lyricism, often explored Bengali village life. As with the Japanese and Americans who were moving away from elitist subjects, Tagore made the same shift in Indian literature toward naturalism—an extreme form of realism "aiming at the closest representation of the facts of existence" (Baker 230). He became the first Asian to win the Nobel Prize in Literature in 1913.

As with Baudelaire, Tagore's prose poems (thought to be influenced by Bengali folk music) often read like miniature stories. Tagore traveled extensively to over thirty countries, including England where earlier he had received his higher education. He impressed many literary icons with his work, among them Ezra Pound and William Butler Yeats. He was in Japan in 1916–17, and is said to have had an influence on fellow Nobel winner Yasunari Kawabata. With the translation of his stories into

Spanish, writers such as Pablo Neruda and Octavio Paz absorbed some of his style.

So while the short short may not have experienced widespread development in India at this time, Tagore's poetic legacy shaped the work of such short short masters as Kawabata and the Latin American magic realists. Today, reading Ana María Shua's *Dream Catcher* flashes is much like reading Tagore's "Fireflies." Published as a collection by MacMillan in 1928, *Fireflies* is made up of many little prose poems originally handwritten on fans and pieces of silk, which, in Tagore's own words, had their origin in Chinese proverbs and in Japanese haiku.

China's Contribution

Despite centuries of cultural isolationism, China was developing its own interest in the short short around the same time. In his translated anthology *The Pearl Jacket and Other Stories* (2008), contributor Shouhua Qi (p. 15) brings to light the vast history and the expansiveness of the genre. What began as early as AD 220–63 in the creation story of Pangu (350 Chinese characters), thrives today as a huge print and online market for stories known most popularly as smoke-long stories. In 1992, China founded its own Microfiction Association.

Contemporary Chinese flash fiction is the combination of its own literary heritage (the movable type printing press was invented in China) with that of other cultures. That China was influenced by such writers as O. Henry and Hemingway is evident in the introduction to the short story "He," by writer and scholar Guo Moruo (1892–1978), found in Qi's anthology: "Lately the short story has become quite in vogue among artists in the West. The shortest has become no more than a dozen lines. Would the piece I've come up with below be worthy of the name at all?" (229). Moruo's story, published in 1920, is 182 English words. Chinese writers still employ O. Henry's twist endings, as witnessed in *The Pearl Jacket*. (Qi's essay in the *Field Guide* reveals more of China's rich history in the short short.)

Yasunari Kawabata: Master of the Short Short

While O. Henry had the largest impact on the short short story in its infancy by virtue of his ability to reach the masses, the truest master of the form was Japanese writer and Nobel Prize winner Yasunari Kawabata (1899–1972). The first prose writer to create countless stories in miniature as a favorite form, he was immersed in the 1920s' Japanese movement toward naturalism, having, as a painter, absorbed cubism, expressionism, and other Euro-stylistic movements.

In the same manner as his fellow Japanese writers, who were concentrating on the common people as their subjects, Kawabata also explored, as in the "floating pictures," characters on the fringe of society. As with Tagore, a writer he had been exposed to, he wrote many of his shorts intentionally as a sort of prose haiku, believing he did not have the ability to be an accomplished poet. He should be credited with being the first to give a name to these miniature stories, "tanagokoro no shosetsu" ("palm-of-the-hand stories"). It's been speculated that he was referring to the fact that the stories could be held in the palm of the hand, but I wonder if he wasn't referring to William Blake's line from the poem "Auguries of Innocence": "Hold infinity in the palm of your hand."

Kawabata was also the first to consistently shape the most basic form of the short—a prose poem that takes a step toward more plot formation. Each of his stories—even the 1927 fabulist story "Yuriko"—is lyrical, full of naturalistic detail with exquisitely measured prose, and is complete. His skill was such that he could distill one of his most popular novels, *Snow Country*, from 200-plus pages down to 11 in the "lite" version, "Gleanings from Snow Country."

One of his translators, J. Martin Holman, says in his introduction to *Palm-of-the-Hand-Stories* (1988), "the plots, though diminutive, are intriguing and memorable." It's of historic note that the first published story in this collection ("A Sunny Place") dates to 1923, before shorts really became established in America. Many more of his shorts saw publication from 1924 on.

The 1920s and the Rise of the American Short Short Story

Ernest Hemingway's In Our Time

In U.S. culture, the Roaring Twenties saw an explosion of artistic creativity in all genres and socioeconomic classes. What the Harper Brothers had started in the nineteenth century—"increasing sales potential of books to mass-culture" (Douglas 14)—was continued and built upon in the new century after the close of World War I. The Book-of-the-Month Club was founded in 1926, tabloid journalism took off, and newspapers and magazines and journals abounded, making publishing New York City's second largest industry, after textiles. Ethnic journals catered to the Jewish community, and to the African American population that was emigrating from the South and starting its own "renaissance." In her book *Mongrel Manhattan* (1995) Ann Douglas notes, "Fifty new black newspapers and periodicals appeared between 1916 and 1921, bringing the number of publications to 500" (324).

In the literary field, some of our best-known writers were making their mark: F. Scott Fitzgerald, Raymond Chandler, Sara Teasdale, Katherine Anne Porter, Hart Crane, Dorothy Parker, H. H. Munro (Saki), Ezra Pound, and a little-known expatriate—Ernest Hemingway. These writers, like their recent predecessors recovering from the Civil War, were now recovering from another war, were being exposed to the new psychological awareness that Freud was making available to the public (*The Interpretation of Dreams* was translated into English in 1913), and were finding a passion for truth (Kate Chopin's "scandalous" work had a revival in the twenties). A friend of Dorothy Parker was quoted as saying that the writer "labored for weeks, sometimes months, over a three-page sketch because . . . 'every word had to be true'" (Douglas 35).

Out of this new "truth culture" came the first U.S. writer to shape an entire collection of what have been called vignettes, sketches, or "interchapters." Ironically, Hemingway wrote it in France in 1924 at the age of 25 "in a few short months of elation" (Douglas 215). That these efforts came "in a burst" (Douglas 216), that he considered modernist Ezra Pound (who had crossed paths with Tagore) his main mentor is, I think, no small coincidence in the evolution of flash fiction, which has often been likened to "flashes" and "explosions." Hemingway also "grudgingly conceded" his debt to Sherwood Anderson (Stevick 64) and admired Rudyard Kipling.

Hemingway's first version of *In Our Time* was published in Paris in 1924, the same year he wrote it, in a print run of just 170. At 32 pages, it consisted of 18 numbered short shorts, some just a half page. Subjects ranged from the World War and the Greco-Turkish War to bullfighting and young love.

The versions that most contemporary readers are familiar with are the 1925 Boni & Liveright U.S. edition and the 1930 Scribner's edition, the former of which Hemingway fleshed out with more developed, longer stories that had appeared in 1923–24 in other publications. He interspersed these with the sketches from the 1924 version, leading to the term "interchapters." While it is purported to have sold only 500 initial copies, it was heavily praised by influential writers F. Scott Fitzgerald and Ford Maddox Ford.

This small book, along with Hemingway's later work, would have more impact on American fiction than any other book in the twentieth century, and on the literary short short (one famous story is titled "A Very Short Story"). Critics have sought to deconstruct his work, in particular the ground-breaking *In Our Time*. It differed not just in structure but in style, moving away from the florid, extravagant pen of the Victorian era. But I think Hemingway's own words on his literary aspirations are explanation enough. In a letter to his father, he writes: "I am trying in all my stories to get the feeling of the actual life across. Not to just depict life . . . but to actually make it alive." This drive to replicate life on paper could be echoed by many of the writers in this collection, such as Nathan Leslie (p. 7), who posits that "flash fiction is *about* ambiguity." In other words, as critic Philip Stevick declares: "Life does not contain plots" (15). It is fragmented, chaotic, and *In Our Time* captures some of that ambiguity.

The Power of the Press, and a Genre Finds Its Niche

The power of the small press and periodicals cannot be underestimated. Many of these aforementioned writers started their own experimental journals, or published in them. And it was in the larger, mass periodicals that the short short story formed, proliferated, and asked to be discovered and named.

The first time the label *short short story* was officially used was in 1926 in *Collier's Weekly*, when the magazine introduced the new feature as "the greatest innovation in short story publication since the work of O. Henry." Soon, other publications followed suit. However, *Liberty* magazine had already been publishing stories with reading times next to the bylines: for example, "4 minutes 30 seconds." These time estimates were getting shorter, and one-page stories were appearing in *Liberty* in the twenties without a label, some years before *Collier's* named them. After *Collier's* stepped out publicly and gave the stories a name and took credit for doing so, *Liberty* gave a September 14, 1929, story by F. R. Buckley its first byline of "a short short story," with no explanation for the change. So while *Collier's* took its place in literary history by naming the genre, *Liberty* still gets a nod for being the first magazine to distill fiction down to a page.

A few months later in November 1929, *Science and Wonder Stories'* editor Hugo Gernsback claimed: "To the best of my knowledge no one has written a short, SHORT science-fiction story up to this time; but I personally believe that there are tremendous possibilities in this particular class of literature. . . . Hence, the present contest." Offering $300 in total prize money for a story between 1,400 and 1,500 words, he begins by saying, "The trend of the times seems to be towards shorter and shorter stories. A few years ago, a short story was anywhere from ten thousand to twenty thousand words. Of late the short, SHORT story has gained ascendancy in a number of magazines, and has opened up a new field for embryo authors" (Vol. 1, no. 6).

He goes on to define a short short story as not running "more than fifteen hundred words; yet the author still finds it possible to tell a coherent tale, into which he packs as much literature and entertainment as does his more ambitious brother. . . ." Because Gernsback wanted to provide a model, he wrote one himself, "The Killing Flash," and published it in that same issue. This appears to be the first SF short short published as such in the United States. As this illustrious beginning suggests, the world of SF has its own rich history in the short short, which in fact spans the globe and could be considered its own genre. Unfortunately, there isn't enough room to expand on its history, which reaches as far back as Sir Francis Bacon (1561–1626).

Even during its inception, the argument over the short's length was not codified. *Liberty* began offering a soon-to-be-famous contest in the thirties for short shorts "not over 1,200 words." Other magazines asked for stories as small as 500 words and as long as 2,000. They paid as high as $1,000 (*Liberty*) and as low as $5, allowing writers to make a living in this genre alone. African American women also had opportunities for publication and profit; for example, *Circuit Magazine*, a Chicago periodical, promoted itself as looking for short shorts of 1,000 words on "domestic life" for "colored women" (Reid and Bordeaux 153).

The fact that there was no consensus on length then or now solidifies the short short as an avenue for experimentation.

"Everybody Seems to Be Writing This Sort of Yarn": The Early Manuals and Anthologies

If writers could make a living on short shorts, then it stands to reason that there were publishers and agents making a living off writers. In 1932, publisher A. Demott Freese of A. D. Freese & Son (Upland, Indiana) commissioned a New England writer, Walter Alderman, to write a 76-page manual titled *Writing the Short, Short Story*. Alderman begins his manual with the statement: "Although but a few years old, the short, short story— or tabloid tale, as it is sometimes called—has made such rapid strides in popular favor that the time is now at hand when it must be accorded its rightful place in the world" (1). He continues by saying that the genre was initially viewed with "good-natured tolerance by the writing fraternity," who believed it more of a fad. However, Alderman reasons, they failed to take into consideration "the modern tendency to briefness and hurry in all places of living, even in reading" (1). He completes his introduction by saying that while there are many types of tabloid tales, "the O. Henry formula has gained a firm hold upon both editors and readers" (3). His manual is not particularly helpful to today's writer, but his chapters on compressing and on the title (see Michael Martone's essay on p. 45) do offer something of value. "Often, . . . the story must be gone over with a 'fine-toothed comb' several times, the 'garden' weeded and reweeded until nothing remains but worth-while blossoms and fresh, green grass" (57).

One agent, Robert Oberfirst (1903–93), dedicated much of his life to selling, writing, and teaching the short short. Together with his brother, Thomas (also an agent), he ran a small short short empire from the 1930s to 1950s.

Oberfirst, who grew up in a farmhouse in Woodbine, New Jersey, and worked as a draftsperson and accountant from 9 to 5, managed his agenting, editing, and writing career on the side. His son, Sheldon, recalls his father typing his stories and articles on his Remington typewriter late into the night.

Oberfirst's love for the short led to a number of publications and long-running anthologies. In 1942, the first full-length book on the short short was published, and it included two of his essays. *Writing the Short Short Story*, edited by *The Writer*'s Sylvia Kamerman and published in Boston by The Writer, Inc., is not very illuminating. The reprinted and commissioned How To articles mostly repeat themselves: writing short shorts is harder than you'd think. But two chapters stand out—Oberfirst's "Cutting Sells a Short Short," which shows the actual cuts in italics that a magazine made before accepting a short for publication, and writer George Freitag's "Writing a Vignette," which discusses the large response he got when he published a 500-word story, "The Lost Land," in *The American Magazine*. It seems readers wanted to "know" what this story was. A prose poem? A sketch? It was shorter than the usual 1,000-plus words they were used to seeing as a short. He decided to call it a vignette: "vignettist," he writes, "is a fancy name for holding your breath while singing" (141). This exchange between Freitag and the public shows how much of an audience there was for such a story, and how they noticed and cared enough to start a dialogue.

This publication lead to Oberfirst's first edited collection published in 1944 by Bruce Humphries, Inc., in Boston. *Technique SELLS the Short-Short* was comprised of additional How To articles Oberfirst had published in *The Writer* from 1939 to 1944, and story examples by a variety of authors from *Liberty, Collier's, Esquire, The New Yorker,* and *Ladies' Home Journal.* The book went through many editions and was used in universities and schools throughout the United States, Canada, England, and Australia. He conducted short short story workshops at the Philadelphia Regional Writers Conference. (Decades later, this conference is still being held and recently included author Randall Brown, p. 68, as a featured presenter on flash fiction.)

Oberfirst's emphasis, as both an agent and a teacher, was on salability.

In Chapter 6 he asks, What makes a short-short salable? He distinguishes between two kinds of shorts—character driven, and plot driven with a twist. He informs that the "smooth paper" magazines "are slowly doing away with the O. Henry type of short-short story with the mechanical, gag-type of ending, and are publishing character short-shorts" (51). He counsels beginners to stick to the O. Henry style: "Beginners usually prefer this type, for their writing is not so smooth and the story will naturally have to depend on a good, strong plot."

In Chapter 1, he warns:

> Everybody seems to be writing this sort of yarn, for it appears to be the easiest form of fictional composition. . . . In reality, the short-short is one of the most difficult forms . . . because it must embody all the technique and consummate skill required in short-story construction 'and then some.' [It] requires tremendous—and skillful—condensation and repression. It must contain all the inherent drama in short-story form. . . . But its technique can be mastered if you understand . . . its fundamental requirements. (9)

Great words for today's writers to adhere to.

Another How To appeared in 1947. This was brought to my attention by Pamelyn Casto, who has also done research on flash. (See her bio on p. 24.) *Writers: Try Short Shorts!* was edited by Mildred I. Reid (author of seven textbooks and grand-niece of The Brothers Grimm) and Delmar E. Bordeaux and published by Bellevue Books in Illinois; it also gives tips on writing in the genre and includes a collection of "Best Short Short Stories by Various Authors." While this book did not prove to be as popular as Oberfirst's, it makes insightful comments in its opening:

> [I]n the decades since 1926, this capsule type of story has been developed into an artistic medium which now demands serious recognition. . . . Some two hundred magazines and newspapers now carry [it] . . . readers of the short short story are thus numbered in the millions.
>
>   . . . No longer is the short short story merely a "trick ending" conundrum. . . . This pill-size story . . . has now been converted

to the serious business of presenting the beauties, the frailties, and the striking nuances of complex human nature. And in this endeavor, . . . has shown itself capable of a facility peculiarly its own. (13–14)

Writers also includes a marketing list at the back of the book. I find it a fascinating time capsule (see fig. 1). Note the magazine titles, locations, requirements, and payments. This list is, additionally, where I discovered the African American and Jewish market for short shorts.

Where To Sell

275 MARKETS FOR SHORT SHORTS

List arranged according to types of stories wanted by various magazines, newspapers, and syndicates, and with word lengths desired and prices paid.

GENERAL

Magazines appealing to the general public and accepting all types of the short short story.

AMERICAN MAGAZINE. 250 Park Ave., New York. 1000 words. All types. Good rates.

THE AMERICAN MERCURY. 570 Lexington Ave., New York. 2000 words. Of general interest. $60.

ATLANTIC MONTHLY. 8 Arlington St., Boston Mass. 1000 words. Shorts must be of superb quality. $20 up.

BEST STORIES. 1746 Broadway, New York. 1000 words. High literary quality. $5-$10.

CANADA WIDE FEATURE SERVICE LIMITED. 249 St. James St., West, Montreal, Canada. 1000 words up. Romance, humor, fantasy, detective, adventure. Prefers stories with a wide appeal, with general background. $10 to $20 up.

COLLIER'S. 250 Park Ave., New York. 1200-1500 words. All types. High rates.

COSMOPOLITAN. 250 Park Ave., New York. 1000-2000 words. All types. Good rates.

COUNTRY GENTLEMAN. Independence Square, Philadelphia. All types. Good plot required. High rates.

THE CRANE PRESS, INC. 1 Madison Ave., New York. Under 1700 words. Stories should have good plots. Moderate rates.

DESTINIES. Box 21, Lake Tahoe, Cal. 1000-2000 words. High literary quality.

139

Fig. 1. Market list for short shorts, opening page, from Mildred I. Reid and Delmar E. Bordeaux, eds., *Writers: Try Short Shorts!* (Rockford, IL: Bellevue Books, 1947), 139. Used by permission of Dr. Robert A. Reid.

In 1948, Oberfirst published the first short short collection by a single author titled *Short-Short Stories*, 28 stories that had appeared from 1937 to 1947 in major syndicate fiction markets under his name and his pen name, Michael Tiff. While they mostly fall under his own rubric of the O. Henry formula, one story, "Red Roses," is the exquisite internal monologue of a female narrator addressing her errant husband. The 2½-page story ends on a twist, but it is more subtle and worthy of the appellation Jennifer Pieroni (p. 65) calls "smart surprise."

Also in 1948, Barthold Fles, a fellow literary agent, published *The Best Short Short Stories from Collier's*. Fles felt the genre reflected the times, and saw patterns in the stories he collected: "the naïve approach of the Twenties with its concern for moral values; the exciting Thirties where new styles of writing were evolving . . . and the sophisticated Forties with its writers very much occupied with the shadow of total war." He felt it was truly an American art form. "It is representative of America and of the era in which we live as the subway, the tabloid, and the automat. It is capsule narrative, and it can be read and digested in a hurry. It is the Twentieth Century approach to literature, although it owes much to the short story form which reached its peak during the Nine-teenth Century [sic]. However, it owes its greatest debt to O. Henry. . ." (11–12).

Following in 1951, *Short Short Stories*, edited by William Ransom Wood, was published. Catering to classroom use (the stories are followed by questions for consideration), it is the first collection devoted solely to the stories themselves. Wood includes such luminaries as Rudyard Kipling, W. Somerset Maugham, and August Strindberg. In the introduction, he states of the stories, "They are always to the point; they make a strong impact on the reader," and goes on to say, "Of all the kinds of imaginative writing, the short short story is most agreeable to the capabilities of high school writers." This foreshadows the beginning trend in writing courses and programs to teach the vignette, or sketch, in the limited time available.

Wood's collection was quickly followed by the first annual short short anthology series of our times, Robert Oberfirst's *Anthology of Best Short Short Stories*, which began in 1952 and ended in 1960 with its eighth volume. These anthologies reprinted short shorts, prize-winning and otherwise, and often included guest essays and shorts, and tips from his *Technique*. The anthologies were a mix of the unknown and the famous. Volume 5 features a guest short by comedian, writer, and songster Steve Allen (whom Oberfirst agented); volume 7 marks the first book appearance of Jack Kerouac's "The Rumbling, Rambling Blues"; volume 8's guest short is by Pinto Colvig, more commonly known as Bozo the Clown; Ray Bradbury appears frequently.

But as the volumes continued, fewer stories were reprinted and more were commissioned. This popular series ended in 1960, and nothing would appear on the short short front until 1968 when Marie de Nervaud Dun published *Harvest of Short Shorts*, a collection of her syndicated stories selected from over 500 that had appeared in such newspapers as the *Chicago Tribune* from 1933 to 1968. They are formulaic in plot and structure, but distinguished by the fact that she is the only woman to have published her own collection of short shorts during much of the twentieth century. Dun's book also shows the extent to which women were publishing during that period on a story-by-story basis, and her stories add weight to what Fles discovered—as they are published over decades, you can see the time's concerns reflected in the plots.

The Short Short's Dormancy

What was happening to the short short story? Why did the Oberfirst series start to commission more and more stories, then end altogether, the collections no longer being churned out? Just as certain industrial inventions of the past led to the greater dissemination and upsurge in print material for the masses, television, which finally took hold with the public around 1948, even more quickly stymied the short short's growth. Periodicals began losing their advertisers and audience to the lure of "the Box." Many magazines slowed production, then folded altogether, and folded fast (*Liberty*, published since 1924, printed its last issue in 1950). Oberfirst continued his anthology series, eventually resorting to self-publishing as a way to provide an outlet for these suddenly deposed short short writers, but never made it to the promised ninth volume.

Gone were the lucrative means for writers to make a living, along with their audience and the readership to do so. It was left to the few magazines that survived, those "smooth" magazines (*The New Yorker, Harper's*) and the small literary magazines, to continue to publish short stories and experimental prose writing. Yet now the short short was solely in the hands of the literary writers, who had been slower to experiment with the structure of the popular O. Henry short. But writers like the lesser-known Mark Schorer (who published *Pieces of Life* in 1977)—or the better-known W. S. Merwin, Donald Barthelme, Jorge Luis Borges, Raymond Carver, Richard Brautigan, and Italo Calvino—continued to find their own place, refusing to follow the status quo. In Merwin's foreword to the 1994 edition of *The Miner's Pale Children*, he states that even with hindsight he is "still not certain what to call the pieces that took shape from that beginning, and almost at once this seemed to me a valuable condition, an advantage that I wanted to retain. . . . I did not want these writings . . . to qualify for membership in some recognizable genre."

This was the voice of a generation speaking. The 1960s and 1970s brought more tumultuous cultural and social changes; citizens and artists in every genre were casting aside labels, values, and any strict adherence to past conventions. Writing became daring, fluid, sexual, and minimalist, and writers played with stream-of-consciousness and altered drug states and returned to old forms, such as fables. The work of many writers like Merwin verged on prose poetry, and to this day the rhetorical arguments continue on the differences between the prose poem and the short short. To that end, two of our contributors explore this subject: Robert Olen Butler and Kim Chinquee on pp. 102 and 109. I don't believe the debate can, or will, ever end—the wall between these forms is too thin.

One writer who achieved acclaim in the seventies, in part by publishing a good number of short shorts in well-respected magazines, is Mark Helprin. Among his many books, *A Dove of the East* (1976) reprints some of his finest very short stories. "Ruin" is perhaps the most well known, written while he was a sophomore at Harvard in the mid-sixties and under the tutelage of Roger Rosenblatt, who asked students to write a story in the style of Hemingway. Many years later, Helprin sent it to *The New Yorker*, which published it in 1975. The irony is that Helprin received some criticism saying he was copying Hemingway (yes, intentionally), down to the featured bull. But the setting and characters and sensibilities all belong to Helprin, who lived in Jamaica for a time.

When asked if he had deliberately written a short short mirroring Hemingway's *In Our Time*, he said no. He was just mirroring Hemingway in general. "Certainly in the world I inhabited in the sixties there was no such thing [as flash] except where it occurred naturally and without identification. But I believe that both the reason for this story and the field itself are one and the same: i.e., when, for the first time, writing fiction was widely 'taught' (it cannot be 'taught') two- and three-page limits were imposed by overburdened instructors . . . I believe this is what Roger did."

This echoes the theory of my own Northport, New York, high school teacher, Kathleen Collins. Collins shaped my writing early on, and the writing of others, such as poet Doug Goetsch (whose first book *Nobody's Hell* includes short prose). She taught us to follow a technique that was before her time. In 1972, also borne of necessity, she began teaching what she called "fragments," or "sketches" or "vignettes," when she had 90 high school students a day, plus 60 others outside school. "I asked for a scene, first person, present tense, that mattered deeply to them. . . . They left out what I called 'school writing' and wrote the heart of the matter. . . . Without having to think about a whole story they could focus on a single moment of intense experience. I figured out that groups of fragments would generate the form of a short story."

She says this was a way to conquer the fear of writing because it was a less intimidating form, as editor William Ransom Wood previously felt. Yet the fragments had enough substance to be a starting point. "The effectiveness of the fragment approach resides in its invitation to the writer not to know anything other than the moment itself mattered, and to 'catch it' with sensory data. . . . My concept was that a group of fragments connected by free association would in themselves generate the form of a short story in which the segments were held to together by emotional glue." This same idea was proposed earlier in regard to Hemingway's *In Our Time*, as some critics felt the story was in the spaces *between* the stories, or sketches. Collins's article "A Fragment Approach to Short Story Writing" appeared in *Teachers & Writers* in 1979. Her mentor was writer Elizabeth Graves, her high school teacher in Seattle, Washington, in 1947–48. Graves asked students to write what she called "deep wells," past experiences that went beyond the "imaginary and/or literary."

These fragments of deep wells that Collins taught could also stand alone, resembling the approach of many contemporary short short writers. During this seventies period, young writer Jayne Anne Phillips (p. 36) emerged. Like Hemingway, she published two limited edition chapbooks of short shorts that would later be interspersed between longer stories in what would go on to be called "an astonishing collection" and a "work of early genius." *Black Tickets* brought the short short back to the foreground in the United States in unique, transcendent prose that retained much of what writers from the naturalist movement on down had been striving to achieve. Phillips emphasizes that while her influences are varied—Katherine Anne Porter, W. S. Merwin, Baudelaire, Rimbaud, Rilke, and others—"they all share a sense of witness, as in, penetration into that deep inner space, a space beyond death, or an afterlife that we associate with timeless meaning/knowledge."

The Short Short Reemerges, Becomes "Flash"

The eighties era, despite being known for its emphasis on money and superficiality, was to become the decade of the rebirth of the literary short short story. In 1981, *Short Short Stories* was published in Canada by Holt, Rinehart and Winston. It was edited by English professors Jack David and Jon Redfern at Centennial College in Ontario, and the idea was born when they came across Hemingway's story "Up in Michigan" (published in 1923 in his first chapbook, *Three Stories and Ten Poems*). This controversial, realistic, raw story of youth and sexuality sparked in the two teachers the idea that they could find other such stories that could be read, analyzed, and discussed in one hour. They looked for stories of no more than 4 pages, "narrative in nature, not merely descriptive, and conventional in the sense that voice, characterization, setting, and symbol were clearly evident in the form." Redfern explained to me that once they found these stories, they were going to call their book *Short Shorts*, then changed it to *Short Short Stories*. They were unaware of the previous history of the label, and "figured we were one of the first to gather such little jewels for the

Canadian educational book market." Their text, offering a short manual of exercises and study suggestions, identifies for the first time a canon of true literary short short writers—Shirley Jackson, John Updike, Octavio Paz, and Julio Cortazár, to name a few—and is still in print.

Almost concurrently, in the United States the rebirth began at a kitchen table in Manhattan. The table owned by writer Irving Howe and his wife, Ilana. The discussion about a small story by Japanese writer Yukio Mishima. The story, "Swaddling Clothes." Clearly influenced by Kawabata, Mishima's slight story centers around the image of a baby wrapped in newspaper. Like these layers of newspaper the narrator must unravel in order to rewrap the baby in flannel, the author layers his story with this image until he ends it in the traditional O. Henryesque manner.

"Swaddling Clothes" inspired the partners to edit *Short Shorts: An Anthology of the Shortest Stories* (Godine, 1982). Included are their own finds—Leo Tolstoy, Anton Chekhov, Sherwood Anderson, Franz Kafka, Jorge Luis Borges, Guy de Maupassant, and many more. In the introduction, Irving Howe writes about the genre he believes he has discovered: "It is fiercely condensed, almost like a lyric poem; it explodes itself to a single, overpowering incident; it bears symbolic weight."

Their limit for selection was rather high by today's standards (2,500 words). And they provided a list of the variations they found common: "One Thrust of Incident, Life Rolled Up, Snap-shot or Single Frame, and Like a Fable"—a similar breakdown to the one Oberfirst promoted in the thirties and forties.

This anthology did not reach a large audience, but it continued to elevate the short short's stature by expanding the canon. And one final, intriguing fact—even though Howe and his wife were unaware, as were David and Redfern, of the previous terminology, the term *short short* is the label they came up with as well; however, I think it is indicative of the direction the short short was taking that Howe uses the word *flash* twice in the introduction and his publisher uses it once on the back jacket copy.

The short short finally was brought back to the masses in 1986 with the first of many anthologies to be edited by Robert Shapard and James Thomas. They, too, were noticing in literary magazines (such as *North American Review* and *Sundog*) that a separate genre seemed to be emerging (or, rather, reemerging). *Sudden Fiction: American Short-Short Stories* gathered works by literary writers past and present. The names we now associate with the contemporary short were included—Pamela Painter (p. 1), Lydia Davis (p. 11), Jayne Anne Phillips (p. 36), Ron Carlson (p. 155), Joyce Carol Oates, Donald Barthelme, and many more.

These multiple anthologies led to an even further shortening of the definition and another new name—*flash*—coined by James Thomas in 1992, which he defined as being between 250–750 words and debuted in *Flash Fiction: 72 Very Short Stories*. Shorter than its predecessor sudden fiction, but longer than Jerome Stern's microfiction, flash is the term the *Field Guide* uses as it applies to the shorter forms and as it has become one of the more popular terms used to reference short shorts in the United States.

The Short Short Today

As author Susana Moore speculates, "style is one way to get to the heart of the matter," and "style itself is a manifestation of what is true." Today's writers, Stuart Dybek (p. 41), Michael Martone (p. 45), and Diane Williams (pp. 114 and 118), are shaping the next generation of flash writers, such as Randall Brown (p. 68), Kim Chinquee (p. 109), Sherrie Flick (p. 121), and Pia Z. Ehrhardt (p. 129), with their unique styles that all serve as vehicles for some truth.

So another technological advance has brought back what television took away: an expanding readership interested in brief styles, and an audience in numbers that rivals and even exceeds the print audience of the late nineteenth century. A new high-tech machine—the computer— has partially lured the audience away from "the Box" and has once again reduced the American reading span still further and allowed for the resurgence in the online magazines that are growing in number almost daily, with blogs also now publishing flash fiction. Flash's brief length makes it perfect for viewing online and on hand-held electronics.

Another modern dilemma: as MFA programs continue to expand, graduating more and more writers, literary magazines have to sift through countless submissions. As an assistant literary magazine editor who used to screen manuscripts in the eighties, and witnessed the shift from messy typewriter manuscripts to polished word-processed ones, I saw the number of multiple submissions rise dramatically. In the old days, when you typed out a story on a Remington, you had one master manuscript, and perhaps one copy if you used blue carbon paper to back it while typing (hence the term *carbon copy*). You could only send out one manuscript at a time, praying it didn't get lost, unless you had easy access to a mimeograph or Xerox machine. Then you had to wait for it to come back. Today, a writer can print out as many copies as she wishes, overwhelming screeners and editors. While it's always unpopular to admit this to struggling writers, reading shorter works becomes timesaving, and soliciting shorter works becomes economical in terms of printing.

Short works are becoming so short that a book such as *Not Quite What I Was Planning: Six-Word Memoirs by Writers Famous and Obscure* was a recent bestseller. We now have 50-word stories (dribbles), 55-word stories (sometimes termed nanofiction, and found, among other places, on an East Indian blog), 100-word stories (drabbles), quick fiction, fast fiction, microfiction, furious fiction, sudden and flash fiction, postcard fiction, napkin fiction (from *Esquire* online), minute-long stories, smoke-long stories, skinny stories, vest-pocket stories and pill-size stories (from the forties), pocket-size stories, palm-size stories, and . . . I am sure there are others, with more to come. These short fictions have become so popular they even made an appearance in *O, The Oprah Magazine* as flash fiction in July 2006, a feature most notable for its publishing of John Edgar Wideman, Stuart Dybek, and Amy Hempel.

What *The Rose Metal Press Field Guide to Writing Flash Fiction* attempts is to take this rather wild-running flash adolescent and settle it down a bit to get a better understanding of its past, present, and future. Some writers might object to the use of *flash* as a label to any writing, but the Press and I feel that it is a genre unto itself; and while labels are often so arbitrary as to be meaningless, the flash writer's intent and outcome are far from being so.

So we asked 25 leading experts in the field of editing, teaching, and writing flash to contribute their ideas—first, on what flash is to them, not in an attempt to find one all-encompassing definition, but to provide the reader with something solid to put their feet on when preparing to approach it themselves. As Irving Howe instructs, "Divisions of genre serve a purpose somewhat like a scaffolding: useful as preliminaries but in the end to be discarded" (xiv–xv). We hope you will feel free to discard what does not sit right with you creatively, but that you will first consider it all.

We then instructed our experts to give some insight into their own approach to flash, and to provide an exercise with an illustrative story example. Many people believe that writing cannot be taught. But as artists, we learn technique, sensibility, and new ways of approach from mentors or artists we admire. Delving into the lives of the short short writers discussed in this introduction, I found it illuminating to see similarities amongst these innovators—a willingness to experiment, an openness to other cultures, an interest in the visual arts, and most of all, a passion for getting at the truth.

Culture is not stagnant—it meets up with other cultures, circles around, travels. As members of different societies, we impact each other in ways that may not be apparent for decades. The short short story has a long, rich history, and many countries and writers share in its evolution. It has survived many social and technological changes, perhaps finding a renewed audience because of its almost adrenaline-inducing ability to capture, in its fragmented brevity, life and some essential truth.

As Shapard and Thomas wrote in their Editor's Note to *New Sudden Fiction*, "Finding a good flash [is] like sighting a comet, all the more glorious for its being rare. . . ." (17). Our goal is to make that find less rare. As you read these essays and experiment with the exercises, remember Mark Helprin and just how far a well-executed exercise can take you. You may not get your flash story published in *The New Yorker*, but if you do what good storytelling is supposed to do, your work will have its own truth, its own "blue pearl of light."

–Tara L. Masih
Editor
Andover, MA, 2009

The Rose Metal Press Field Guide to Writing

FLASH FICTION

Pamela Painter

YOU AND THE PIANO BENCH

I suspect that quite a few writers have spent time on a piano bench, and those who have not might instead have put in hours plucking the strings of a guitar, or working to acquire the perfect embouchure for their horn, trombone, or flute. And playing exercises. In this essay, I'd like to make a case for the value of writing exercises—that they can be as important to a writer as exercises are to an aspiring musician or singer. When my coauthor Anne Bernays and I were in the process of soliciting student examples for our book *What If? Writing Exercises for Fiction Writers*, some of our graduate students voiced the opinion that writing exercises are artificial and only valuable for beginners. Now, at the end of each semester, our students are converts. They are also better readers because they have seen that many of our exercises come from noting how a writer has accomplished a particularly difficult task. Fitzgerald and Hemingway used to write letters to each other in which they pointed out the "tricks" they learned from Conrad, Kipling, and Oscar Wilde, among others. But how do writing exercises work, and how can they be put to good use? Here I'll be talking from experience—experience I hope others will soon replicate in search of their flash fiction stories.

The leader of one of the first writing groups I joined began our evening

Pamela Painter, from Pittsburgh, Pennsylvania, is the author of two story collections, *The Long and Short of It* (1995) and *Getting to Know the Weather* (reissued in 2008), and is the coauthor of *What If? Writing Exercises for Fiction Writers* (3rd ed., 2009), which includes a section of flash fiction exercises. Stories have appeared in *Atlantic, Harper's, Kenyon Review, Ploughshares*, and *Quick Fiction*, and in all the major flash fiction anthologies, and have won three Pushcart Prizes and *Agni*'s John Cheever Award for Fiction. Painter lives in Boston where she teaches in the Writing, Literature, and Publishing Program at Emerson College, a program she has helped shape through her influential revision classes and her promotion of the short short story form.

meetings with an exercise. For one exercise he set banjo music playing on the stereo, put a penny on a table, and passed around a grainy photograph of two eyes peering through the wooden slats of a boarded-up window. My story was about a bored teenage girl sitting on an orange crate in a country store. There is a penny under her shoe—and she knows that only the boy watching her through the boarded-up window has seen her slide it there. Everyone in the group used the same details, but our stories were totally different—of course. Because each of us has a unique imagination, voice, and vision. (A few years later, my story "Close to Home" gave the title to that year's *Intro Awards* anthology, edited by the late George Garrett.)

Almost always, the beginning paragraphs that I wrote in response to an exercise in the first five minutes of that workshop became a story. I soon realized that there was nothing artificial about an exercise—except the origin of the prompt. What you write in response to that prompt becomes organically your own with the first words you write after taking in the instructions. You are making decisions about point of view, tense, tone, setting, and sometimes playing games with yourself.

Exercises teach you how to hear the outside world as a sea of prompts, a sea of exercises for potential stories. Doing exercises trains you to appreciate the value of an overheard conversation, a newspaper story, or a friend's anecdote, and how it might be used—should your friend respond favorably and generously to your importuning request to be given the "story."

Exercises are, well, exercise—a limbering up of your imagination and the language that renders story. They help you to set in motion the shape of story, the "what if?" that might be applied to a particular set of circumstances or a line of dialogue, or even just a few words that can lock a story into place.

My students saw this process in person during a short short workshop I taught at the Fine Arts Work Center in Provincetown. On the second day, I was opening a bottle of water I believed was "still" but was, in fact, seltzer. In seconds, the front of my T-shirt was soaked. Absolutely sopping wet. The man to my right hurried to retrieve paper towels, handed a bunch to me, and then began mopping the floor. I applied a few towels to the front of my shirt and, because I was so thoroughly drenched, I peeled the front of my shirt away from my skin, and positioned a few paper towels underneath. Then I patted myself down. The class was a little startled, and someone remarked, "Inside job." We all laughed, and I said, "See, see . . . there's the title of a story. The story of a young woman or man at a party who takes part in the mopping up. If it is the woman's point of view, then she instructs or allows the man to do it. Or perhaps it is the man's point of view, and he is a bit forward in making it an inside job."

In my mind, those words immediately became the title of a flash fiction story—(Here, dear reader, I stopped writing this essay to actually write the story. Because if you "tell" stories to your friends or to your seatmate on an airplane, or to anyone, the pressure to write the story is soon dissipated and the story will never get written.)

OK, I just wrote the story and now I'm back. Twenty minutes and 300 words—and I have a first draft of a story titled "Inside Job," imperfect and in need of revision, below.

Inside Job

The party at the Associate Chair's home was in full swing, which meant that almost every bottle of bourbon, vodka, and Scotch had been breached, alarmed pets and small children in pjs had been relegated to the stairs, and the music was too haphazard to invite accusations. Discretion about the college's most recent search was also being breached, though in euphemisms that Marla declined to follow. "Better that way, given the litigious nature of academe," her husband would have said had he been standing soberly nearby instead of chatting up the new gaggle of graduate students, one in particular clearly the chosen one for his next indiscretion. Marla herself was still sober enough to realize that she was going to have to cut him loose—or embark on an indiscretion of her own. It made her a bit more attentive (almost for the first time) to her husband's colleague, Jeremy, who often settled near her when a party reached the settling-in stage of guttering candles and lounging, slouching sloth. Her husband was now on the Victorian love seat with the young woman whose long hair was so straight she surely ironed it. Oddly, bits were softly attached to her husband's shoulder. "Water," Marla said, and together she and Jeremy went off to the kitchen to look for bottled water. Belatedly, they understood seltzer. Or rather Marla did as seltzer burst forth and drenched the front of her blouse. In seconds she was soaked, sopping wet. Sodden. Jeremy unfurled a roll of paper towels and gallantly set about mopping and patting her blouse. "No," she said, and took his towel-filled hand. She lifted her blouse and placed his hand here and there. Their eyes met and his hand slowed as he found less and less water. But more of her.

Believe me, I would not have written a story about getting drenched with seltzer without those words *inside job*. I "heard" a story when my student said those two words.

Structure can also be the origin of an exercise. Former student and now novelist Jane Berentson sent me an email of a Vietnamese restaurant review she'd found pinned up on her office's bulletin board. The structure of the review went like this: *He said* _____. *She said*_____. *He said*_____. *She said* _____. It continued in that contrapuntal way for a long paragraph. My student went on to say that she thought it might make a good flash fiction exercise. Indeed. It is the prompt I have contributed at this essay's end, together with a student example.

And last week, a friend, in utter disbelief that I did not know of this book, gave me poet and novelist Raymond Queneau's *Exercises in Style*, translated by Barbara Wright. Queneau was one of the founders of *Oulipo* (Ouvroir de littérature potentielle), a group of French writers and mathematicians who wrote using what they called "constraints." Queneau's book plays a game with structure—it is an exercise or constraint he devised for himself. Wright, in her preface, notes that the idea for *Exercises* came to Queneau after attending a concert. She says, "What particularly struck Queneau about this piece [Bach's *The Art of the Fugu*] was that, although based on a rather slight theme, its variations 'proliferated almost to infinity.' It would be interesting, he thought, to create a similar work of literature."

The first story in *Exercises*, "Notation," is told by a narrator who witnesses a confrontation between two men on a crowded bus, and who later observes one of the men being advised by a friend to put another button on his overcoat. Queneau retells this "slight" tale 98 other ways. One variation, "Double Entry," doubles everything up: "Towards the middle of the day and at midday"; "thin neck and skinny windpipe." Another variation, "Telegraphic," takes the form of a telegram: "BUS CROWDED STOP MAN LONGNECK…" Yet another variation is all exclamations: "Goodness! Twelve o'clock! time for the bus!" and so on. Buy this book.

Meanwhile, when talking to students about the value of exercises, I often use as example the musical compositions that a beginning piano student might play. After not practicing for decades, I recently had occasion to play on a magnificent piano. I would have preferred to move right along to Gershwin's *Three Preludes* or a Beethoven sonata but I first had to return to the *Czerny Exercises* and Bach's *Two and Three Part Inventions*. No pianist thinks that time spent with the *Inventions* is lost because in themselves they are splendid music—and the student of writing should take writing exercises just as seriously, as time well spent.

The wonder of a flash fiction story exercise in particular is that it can lead to a complete story, a story capable of achieving perfection.

⸺✸⸺

A FLASH FICTION PROMPT

"He said/She said"

Write a story that is 250 to 500 words long. Use the structure of alternating voices. *He said:* _____. *She said:* _____.
He said: _____. *She said:* _____. And so on.

The two "characters" should disagree about an issue or subject and their dialogue should have a subtext, an emotional truth that is operating on a deeper and perhaps hidden level. As you will see, the story example, by a student I met at a writers conference in Ourey, Colorado, is not about misplaced keys.

A STORY EXAMPLE

Without a Second Thought

He says: Just put the keys in the same place every time. *She says:* It's not that easy. *He says:* Retrace your steps. *She says:* It's better if

I try to remember what I was thinking about. *He says:* Let's start at the front door. *She says:* It was dinner I was thinking about, salmon baked in foil. *He says:* Let's walk to the kitchen. *She says:* I was fumbling with the keys, my hands full of groceries, thinking how old it gets being locked out with you already home. *He says:* It's for security. *She says:* They're still in the deadbolt. *He says:* Every time, just put them on the hook behind the front door, on the counter next to the pile of old bills and letters, on the table next to the photograph from the day we spent at the lake, that time you wouldn't jump in the water because you said there were snakes even though I promised you there weren't. *She says:* The last place I'd think to look is on a hook behind the front door. *He says:* The problem is you don't believe me. It's careless. *She says:* It's a habit.

—Kathleen Blackburn, student

Nathan Leslie

THAT "V" WORD

Speculations

We can only speculate how and why flash fiction has risen to prominence—perhaps it is as simple as decreased attention spans and the rise of online literary magazines (the computer lending itself to the quick read rather than to long-term immersion). In a sense, however, it doesn't particularly matter how we got to this place of prominence; what's important is that we're here. And yet some of the literate populace still demean flash fiction as "slight," "minor," as "just a vignette." I beg to differ. I think a great work in this form can, in fact, yield quite a bit more than the hundred thousand words of a mediocre novel. And the writing of flash fiction takes great care and attention to detail; it doesn't suffer fools. This is a slop-free zone.

"Just a Vignette"

In creative writing classes "vignette" is often a four-letter word. If student A describes student B's short story as a "vignette," he or she often means that the story in question lacks a clear plot. The connotation of "vignette" is that it implies a formless blob of a story, the kind of story Jerome Stern

Nathan Leslie has published six short story collections, five of which feature flash fiction: *Rants & Raves* (2002), *A Cold Glass of Milk* (2003), *Drivers* (2005), *Believers* (2006), and *Reverse Negative* (2006). His short stories, essays, and poems have appeared in numerous literary magazines. He is fiction editor for *The Pedestal Magazine* online, which often publishes very short fiction, and is series editor for *The Best of the Web* anthologies, which began in 2008 (Dzanc Books). Born in Minnesota and raised in Maryland, Leslie now lives in Virginia where he teaches composition, literature, and creative writing at Northern Virginia Community College. In addition, he teaches flash fiction workshops for Writers at the Beach and elsewhere. "Welcome to the short fiction revolution" is the greeting on his website, www.nathanleslie.com.

warns us against in *Making Shapely Fiction*—the bathtub story, the hobos in space story—a story that, at best, goes in circles, if anywhere at all. According to both *The American Heritage Dictionary* and *Webster's*, a vignette is "(a) a short descriptive literary sketch" or "(b) a brief incident or scene." With one sole exception, any writer of flash fiction should actually *aspire* to these traits—short, descriptive, literary, brief, incident, scene. These are all positive attributes of flash fiction. The only word in question is *sketch*.

Sketchy

When we hear the word *sketch* we think of an artist's charcoal impression, a study for a larger work. And "impression" was the nasty four-letter modifier used to describe Manet, Monet, and the rest of the Impressionist painters. But what was once a four-letter word became an honorable calling card. Just as there was nothing wrong with their original works, there is nothing inherently wrong or ineffective with a work of flash fiction that provides a sketch. A writer clearly has the option to fill the gaps by more fully dramatizing the action. Yet flash fiction at its best has ambiguity on its side; it doesn't shrink from mystery, it embraces it. If a reader desires full dramatization of every dramatizable moment, he or she should read a novel, which is about expansion; flash fiction is *about* ambiguity. Flash fiction is about a singular moment, a slice of life, a sketch.

Socks

One work of flash fiction I often teach in my undergraduate creative writing classes is "The Sock" by Lydia Davis. Reprinted in the classic flash fiction anthology *Sudden Fiction*, "The Sock" portrays in intimate detail the internal struggles of an unnamed female narrator whose ex-husband arrives to visit along with his new wife and his mother. Awkward. Over the course of the story Davis portrays the narrator's dealings with her ex-husband and ex-mother-in-law, as they proceed to make themselves comfortable in her home before going out for dinner. That's the extent of the plot. The story concludes with two breathless paragraphs that detail the narrator's domestic memories of her husband in his socks. In this story the sock becomes a stand-in for what her husband has left behind—

the narrator. She's still clearly hung up on him, and yet she doesn't exactly grab the bull by the horns—she expresses herself passively, allows her ex-husband to walk all over her. Inevitably, my students have a wide-ranging reaction to this story. Some students are frustrated by the narrator and think she is spineless, a woman who needs to stand up to her husband and move on; others find her relatable, compassionate, kind, sympathetic—despite the pain it causes her. I teach the story as an example of a successful work of flash fiction (and fiction in general)—in part because of its expert use of ambiguity. Davis never tips her hand as to how we should react to the narrator or her dilemma; we have to read between the lines and come to our own conclusions. More to the point, "The Sock" is a classic example of a vignette. Nothing really "happens," per se. The narrator and the family she was once a part of spend an evening together. The "action," so to speak, is entirely internal, beneath the surface, intimate. The story revolves around the sense of loss the narrator experiences, rather than some external event. No other individual in the world other than the narrator would possess a sense of the magnitude of the sock dangling carelessly from her husband's back pocket. Davis captures a compelling and contradictory character with precision and pathos. Her slice of life is a slice that bears repeat reading.

A Taxonomy

If I had to provide a taxonomy of flash fiction, I'd say one could break down the form into five primary types—the monologue ("The Walled Garden" by Peter Taylor), the tale (Aimee Bender is a recent proponent of this), the individual scene (the most common type of flash fiction), the snapshot story (small glimpses of time accumulating into a larger picture—think "The Hit Man" by T. C. Boyle), and the experiment (think Donald Barthelme among many others). All five types are really vignettes at heart—brief moments in time. The pretension of novels is that by containing a "plot" they are somehow closer to the human experience, somehow more real. Au contraire. *My* day-to-day experience is often plotless; I suspect this is the case with the majority. Many novels seem to fail in the last 50 pages by trying too hard to be tidy, to wrap up events within a tight, plotted package. Lived experience often doesn't work this way (perhaps this is why novels sell better than short fiction—they are closer to entertainment). Life is ambiguity, not serendipitous plotting. In this way, flash fiction is actually *truer* to life than other literary forms. This is not to say nothing happens in flash fiction—just that small adjustments or revelations work better on the small stage than do major events.

Ice Melting on a Stove

I preach to my students that to write quality flash fiction one needs to actually embrace the concept of the vignette, to loosen one's bond to the "tightly" plotted story concept. Joyce Carol Oates compared flash fiction to Frost's classic definition of a poem—"a structure of words that consumes itself as it unfolds, like ice melting on a stove." This is useful. By focusing on language, scene, voice, and character, my students often find themselves writing compelling and effectively ambiguous stories rather than cloyingly serendipitous and artificial ones. By doing so they learn that in flash fiction:

- Accomplishing one clear goal is of utmost importance. In flash fiction the singular impression is everything.

- Hemingway's Iceberg Principle, and minimalist writing overall, can work wonders—understatement and purposeful ambiguity are vital. Trust the reader to fill in gaps. As Hemingway writes in his nonfiction book *Death in the Afternoon*, "If a writer of prose knows enough about what he is writing about he may omit things that he knows and the reader, if the writer is writing truly enough, will have a feeling of those things as strongly as though the writer had stated them."

- Every word bears weight. Thus, lyrical writing tends to work well in this form.

- Imagery is of the utmost importance. In a genre that works best via implication, use words that pack a punch.

- Many works of flash fiction can employ a sudden twist, turn, or realization. This doesn't necessarily imply a grand epiphany, but a smaller internal adjustment is often required.

- Irony is helpful; playing against expectations works.

- Beginning in the middle saves precious time and space.

- Last but not least, length restrictions can bring out great art. In the afterword of *Sudden Fiction* Stuart Dybek writes: "Part of the fun of writing them is the sense of slipping between the seams. Within the constraint of their small boundaries the writer discovers great freedom. In fact, their very limitations of scale also demand unconventional strategies. . . ." Hear, hear.

Stand Tall

As flash fiction writers, perhaps we need a catchier calling card than "Vignetteist"—something like Impressionist, with perhaps a few less syllables. So write your vignette; write your slice of life. Be proud of your ability to capture (and capture well) one discrete moment in time. What else is there?

A FLASH FICTION EXERCISE

Write a story that revolves around an article of clothing in some way—a hat, a shirt, a suede jacket, underwear, what have you. The article of clothing doesn't necessarily need to be the primary focus of attention, but it will hopefully act as a trigger to or as a symbol of your imagination, which should help spur a vignette that captures something of greater meaning.

A STORY EXAMPLE

The Sock

My husband is married to a different woman now, shorter than I am, about five feet tall, solidly built, and of course he looks taller than he used to and narrower, and his head looks smaller. Next to her I feel bony and awkward and she is too short for me to look her in the eye, though I try to stand or sit at the right angle to do that. I once had a clear idea of the sort of woman he should marry when he married

again, but none of his girlfriends was quite what I had in mind and
this one least of all.

They came out here last summer for a few weeks to see my son,
who is his and mine. There were some touchy moments, but there
were also some good times, though of course even the good times
were a little uneasy. The two of them seemed to expect a lot of ac-
commodation from me, maybe because she was sick—she was in
pain and sulky, with circles under her eyes. They used my phone
and other things in my house. They would walk up slowly from the
beach to my house and shower there, and later walk away clean
in the evening with my son between them, hand in hand. I gave
a party, and they came and danced with each other, impressed
my friends and stayed till the end. I went out of my way for them,
mostly because of our boy. I thought we should all get along for his
sake. By the end of their visit I was tired.

The night before they went, we had a plan to eat out in a Vietnamese restaurant with his mother. His mother was flying in from
another city, and then the three of them were going off together the
next day, to the Midwest. His wife's parents were giving them a big
wedding party so that all the people she had grown up with, the
stout farmers and their families, could meet him.

When I went into the city that night to where they were staying, I
took what they had left in my house that I found so far: a book, next
to the closet door, and somewhere else a sock of his. I drove up to
the building, and I saw my husband out on the sidewalk flagging me
down. He wanted to talk to me before I went inside. He told me his
mother was in bad shape and couldn't stay with them, and he asked
me if I would please take her home with me later. Without thinking I
said I would. I was forgetting the way she would look at the inside of
my house and how I would clean the worst of it while she watched.

In the lobby, they were sitting across from each other in two
armchairs, these two small women, both beautiful in different
ways, both wearing lipstick, different shades, both frail, I thought
later, in different ways. The reason they were sitting here was that
his mother was afraid to go upstairs. It didn't bother her to fly in an

airplane, but she couldn't go up more than one story in an apartment building. It was worse now than it had been. In the old days
she could be on the eighth floor if she had to, as long as the windows
were tightly shut.

Before we went out to dinner my husband took the book up to
the apartment, but he had stuck the sock in his back pocket without
thinking when I gave it to him out on the street and it stayed there
during the meal in the restaurant, where his mother sat in her black
clothes at the end of the table opposite an empty chair, sometimes
playing with my son, with his cars, and sometimes asking my husband and then me and then his wife questions about the pepper-
corns and other strong spices that might be in her food. Then after
we all left the restaurant and were standing in the parking lot he
pulled the sock out of his pocket and looked at it, wondering how it
had got there.

It was a small thing, but later I couldn't forget the sock, because
here was this one sock in his back pocket in a strange neighborhood way out in the eastern part of the city in a Vietnamese ghetto,
by the massage parlors, and none of us really knew this city but we
were all here together and it was odd, because I still felt as though
he and I were partners, we had been partners a long time, and I
couldn't help thinking of all the other socks of his I had picked up,
stiff with his sweat and threadbare on the sole, in all our life together
from place to place, and then of his feet in those socks, how the skin
shone through at the ball of the foot and the heel where the weave
was worn down; how he would lie reading on his back on the bed
with his feet crossed at the ankles so that his toes pointed at different
corners of the room; how he would then turn on his side with his feet
together like halves of a fruit; how, still reading, he would reach down
and pull off his socks and drop them in little balls on the floor and
reach down again and pick at his toes while he read; sometimes he
shared with me what he was reading and thinking, and sometimes he
didn't know whether I was there in the room or somewhere else.

I couldn't forget it later, even though after they were gone I
found a few other things they had left, or rather his wife had left

them in the pocket of a jacket of mine—a red comb, a red lipstick, and a bottle of pills. For a while these things sat around in a little group of three on one counter of the kitchen and then another, while I thought I'd send them to her, because I thought maybe the medicine was important, but I kept forgetting to ask, until finally I put them away in a drawer to give her when they came out again, because by then it wasn't going to be long, and it made me tired all over again just to think of it.

—Lydia Davis, from *PEN Short Story Collection*

Shouhua Qi

OLD WINE IN NEW BOTTLES?
Flash Fiction from Contemporary China

Flash Fiction, or *wei xing xiao shuo*, as it is known in China today, also goes by the name of Minute Story, Pocket-Size Story, Palm-Size Story, and, perhaps most evocatively and, in my opinion, most accurately (for China at least)—Smoke-Long Story, which promises to let the reader relish the sights and sounds of an entire make-believe world before he or she has time to finish one delicious cigarette.

Deep Roots in Native Soil

Although the name has a ring of novelty to it, flash fiction in China can be traced as far back as the creation myths of Nuwa (350 BC?), Fuxi, and Pangu. The story of Pangu, a legendary godlike giant, which first appeared in written form during the Three Warring States period (AD 220–263), has a word count of 350 in Chinese. It is "flash fiction" all right. If squeezed hard, it may even fit the "microfiction" label. Yet there was nothing "micro" about the way Pangu created the world, separating *yin* and *yang* with a swing of his great axe, standing between Heaven and Earth to uphold the sky, with such inspiration, courage, and force that we are still experiencing the ramifications today. It took Pangu no less than 18,000 years

A native of Nanjing (Nanking), China, *Shouhua Qi* (pronounced "Chee") came to the United States in 1989 with a fellowship to complete his doctoral degree. He is the author of 15 books, including *Red Guard Fantasies and Other Stories* (2007). *When the Purple Mountain Burns* (2005) was one of China's "Top 100 WWII-Themed Books," recommended to commemorate the sixtieth anniversary of the Second World War. Currently associate professor of English at Western Connecticut State University, he recently translated and edited *The Pearl Jacket and Other Stories: Flash Fiction from Contemporary China* (2008), from which the excerpts in this essay were taken. Because modern Chinese flash fiction writers are not readily available in English translation, his goal is to help bring these authors and stories to a wider audience.

to complete his feat, but the story can be told in the pintsize space of a few hundred words.

And it would take more than two full millennia for flash fiction to evolve to where it is today—as a hot, *white-hot,* important literary genre. Along the way many great writers have tried their hands at this story-telling form: Pu Songling (1640–1715), Wu Jingzi (1701–54), Cao Xueqing (1715–63), among others. Many of the 400 or so stories in Pu's *Strange Tales from a Chinese Studio* are only a couple of hundred words long. In one story, titled "Stir-Fry," a certain scholar finds to his chagrin that his wife has just served to guests a dildo he had acquired on the sly when taking the civil service exams in the provincial capital. He had taken care to keep the rattan dildo out of sight by letting it soak in a bowl of water under the bed:

> "You foolish woman! How could you think of serving such a thing to our guests!"
>
> "I was wondering why you never gave me a recipe for it," replied his perplexed wife. "It was such a nasty-looking thing! I had no idea what it was. All I could think of doing was chopping it up into little pieces and stir-frying it . . ."
>
> He proceeded to tell her what the "nasty-looking thing" really was, and the two of them had a good laugh about it.
>
> This man went on to become a man of rank. His good friends still joke with him about this story.[1]

And quite a racy story, indeed.

Burgeoning Afresh in the Early Twentieth Century

Fast forwarding to the twentieth century we find Guo Moruo (1892–1978), one of the most important modern Chinese writers, musing aloud about flash fiction in the introduction to a story titled "He," published in 1920: "Lately the short story has become quite in vogue among artists in the West. The shortest has no more than a dozen lines. Would the piece I've

---

[1] Pu Songling, *Strange Tales from a Chinese Studio,* trans. and ed. John Minford (New York: Penguin, 2006) 452.

come up with below be worthy of the name at all?" He goes on to tell the story of a Mr. K who, on his way home from purchasing firewood on a moonlit evening, runs into a former classmate who invites him to a mutual friend's place:

> "No. Visiting with firewood in my arms?"
> "Don't want to come and have fun?"
> "No, I've got to go home."
> They went separate ways at H Shrine. He went on home murmuring his own poems.

An apparently nonsensical story unless one is hell-bent in finding sense, or theme, by giving the short text (182 words in English) a good probe under a strong magnifying glass.

"Theme," though, *is* the title of another 1920s story by Lu Xun (1881–1936), the standard-bearer of modern Chinese literature. In this story of under 200 words, the first-person narrator asks his schoolmaster how to establish theme in writing. To illustrate his point the schoolmaster uses the impossible situation of finding the proper thing to say at a newborn baby's 100-day celebration:

> "To say the child will die is telling the truth. To say the child will be wealthy or powerful is telling a lie. But the one lying was richly rewarded while the one telling the truth was beaten."
> "I don't want to tell lies, and I don't want to be beaten, either. So, master, what should I say?"
> "Okay, then, you'll have to say, 'This child! Oh my! How. . . . indeed! Ha ha ha! Hee hee hee! Hee hee hee!'"

That "hearty" laugh should send eerie, bone-chilling echoes across all Orwellian dystopias, Chinese and otherwise, past or present.

Full Flowering in Contemporary China

The apparent absence of good flash fiction for decades since Guo Moruo and Lu Xun can be attributed to China's turbulent modern history. The Great Proletariat Cultural Revolution of 1966–76 nearly wiped Chinese literature and art off the map. Then, in the 1980s, flash fiction reemerged on China's literary scene with a vengeance. Taking root in fertile native soil and drawing nourishment from outside influences, especially the influx of modern and postmodern Western literature translated into Chinese since the late 1970s, flash fiction quickly matured as a literary form. The birth of the Microfiction Association of China in 1992, and the popularity of literary journals devoted to such fiction exclusively (*The Journal of Microfiction, The Journal of the Short-Short Story*) attest to the recent popularity of flash fiction in China. New technologies, such as text messaging, blogging, and extensive (though still tightly controlled) use of the Internet, make it possible for millions of people to dally with writing their own stories and "publishing" them to family, friends, and complete strangers. There is instant satisfaction when the desire to be heard, and to be known ("Sir, I exist!"), is met with a few strokes of the keyboard. Imagine a nation of tens of millions of storytellers!

Although each of the thousands of flash fiction stories published each year in China is unique in its own way, some broad categories can be drawn about them in terms of subject matter and style.

Pulsing with China Today

A great many, if not most, of the stories have their finger on the pulse of what is going on in China today; they are stories of simple, ordinary, sometimes confused folks caught in the unsettling drama of profound socioeconomic and cultural transformations: an illiterate peasant who keeps a daily vigil outside an office window hoping to sell his smelly, tattered wool coat to a rich foreign tourist; a "hooliganish" young man who is misunderstood for his attempt at being father to an abandoned baby; a country girl who finds the outside world too much for her but feels equally lost when she returns to her village; a rustic war veteran who is condemned to a Sisyphean quest for the concerned government departments to receive the benefits to which he is fully entitled.

Using History to Satirize Here and Now

Many writers, though, turn to China's historical past for inspiration. While many are content with telling straight "historical" stories, others don't want to stop there. Their "historical" stories may be traditional in narrative mode and appear to be politically innocuous enough, but embedded in them are critical barbs that are hard to miss. In a 2004 story, titled "Cat and Mouse Play," the historical lesson the General taught his Second-in-Command may, ostensibly, have to do with China's distant imperial past. However, the story's subtext, its pungent satire directed at the political life of modern China—especially given what Mao Zedong did to his Long March comrades-in-arms during the Cultural Revolution—becomes apparent when one considers the fact that "Using Ancient History to Satirize the Here and Now" has been a favorite trope among Chinese writers (and dissident intellectuals) since time immemorial.

Telling Old Stories Anew

Some writers choose to treat their historical source material rather playfully and give well-known, classic stories a postmodern twist with delightful, refreshing effect. Such is the case of "To Kill the Sister-in-Law" by Jia Pingwa, a writer known in the West for such work as *Defunct Capital* (banned in China when it was first published in 1993). Jia draws from the classic novel *Water Margin:* the story of Wu Song (the tall, handsome hero famed for having killed a fierce tiger with his bare hands) avenging the death of his midget brother, who has been poisoned by his sister-in-law Pan Jinlian and her rakehell lover. In the original story the heroic, righteous Wu Song, who had earlier rebuffed Pan's adulterous advances, never wavers for a second in meting out justice. Jia, however, makes Wu Song agonize, *aloud*, between his resolve for revenge and the tantalizing beauty under his sword.

Relishing the "Strange" and "Extraordinary"

As if driven by a desire to escape from the humdrum of everyday life, some writers chase after the "strange" and "extraordinary" in oral history, folklore, or their own high-strung imagination: a male obstetrician whose unusually small hands spell both his fortune and his demise; an old, hunchbacked gold washer who finally strikes gold (a glittering piece the size of a nut!), but unknowingly lets someone else walk away with it; a mysterious merchant who rocks an entire town out of its wits by collecting wills from folks on their death beds; a paranoiac king whose very life hangs on the dance of a pair of pearls; a gang of wacky river bandits whose most lethal weapons are bees, and so on. Is there anything more in such stories than the sigh, the chuckle, or the inarticulate wonderment they have to offer? Anything allegorical, provocative (covertly political), underneath the façade of the "strange" and "extraordinary"? Readers will have to decide for themselves.

Questing for "the Philosopher's Stone"

To provoke thought is certainly among the effects intended by writers of another group of stories. These stories focus on a moment (existential?), a phenomenon, an occurrence, or simply an unlikely dialogue, to shine some fierce light on human nature and the nature of being: How a precious stone from the beach brings a man joy, fortune, and doom; how the 20 cents or so extra a tourist has paid for a bag of tea at the mountain top rattles his otherwise complacent world; how two fish denounce each other for not being a true, loyal friend; how two old men, sunbathing on a winter day, argue over whether the bird in the sky is a hawk. Indeed a rock, a cloud, and the most inconsequential thing under the sky can inspire some serious yet delightful philosophizing by flash fiction writers.

Flash fiction is just as hot in Taiwan, Hong Kong, Macau, and among Chinese writers and readers elsewhere in the world. Stories by the "overseas" writers enrich the thematic, emotional, and stylistic tapestry of Chinese flash fiction. If the *yang* force pulses restlessly in stories from mainland China, the *yin* force in "overseas" stories prove equally irresistible with their well-tuned sensitivity, ease of flow, and a disquieting yet satisfying sensation that lingers long after the reading.

Whether drawing from the here and now of contemporary China or from the nation's collective memory, whether traditional, experimental, or avant-garde in their narrative modes, the best of Chinese flash fiction not only captures the pulse of life of a given time and place, but also has something to say about the human condition, which should resonate with readers everywhere. Honest truth, big or small, emotional as well as intellectual, gives life to each story and makes the minutes one spends with it a delightful, illuminating experience.

⌒⁄ℓ⌒

A FLASH FICTION EXERCISE

Wang Renshu (1901–72, pen name Ba Ren) was an important Chinese writer, literary critic, editor, publisher, and historian. Ambassador to Indonesia from 1950 to 1952, throughout his career Wang authored eight short story collections, five novels, and numerous essay collections, reviews, critiques, plays, and translations of literature from English, French, and Japanese; his writing career was cut short when he was persecuted during the Chinese Cultural Revolution (1966–77) for his political views and, hence, denied the right to publish.

The pathos of his 1936 story "Blowfish" lies in its effective use of irony (situational irony, to be exact) as a literary device to dramatize the plight of its protagonist and his family: the incongruity between the protagonist's anguished desire to end his family's suffering from hunger by killing them with poison fish, and the outcome of his action. The O. Henryesque twist at the end of the story (popular with many Chinese flash writers) drives home the pathos of the story and the plight of the family.

For this exercise, follow these two steps:

1. Describe five story possibilities (plots, if you will); each, in a sentence or two, should involve the kind of situational irony as embodied in "Blowfish." The main character desires something, acts out the desire, and the action leads to an unintended outcome, or outcomes, for better or worse.

2. Choose one of these five plots to develop into a story of no more than 500 words.

A STORY EXAMPLE
Blowfish

He learnt about this from someone and decided to make the move.

Somehow he got a basket of blowfish and carried it home quietly.

Three successive years of disastrous harvest left him with barely enough grain to pay the landowner and little to feed his family of five. It had been excruciatingly difficult for him, all alone, to pull the family through from last winter to early spring. Now, all that was left was hunger.

But how could he let his family suffer hunger?

When his family saw him back with a full basket, they all jumped for joy, as if he were an angel.

The kids met him at the door, half dancing.

"Pop, Pop! What is it? Let's eat it!"

At this tears welled up in his eyes.

"Eat," he mumbled, terrified by his own voice, terrified for the lives of his kids; his heart nearly froze.

He told his wife to cook the fish and then left on the pretext of an errand. Not that he didn't want to die himself, but that he didn't want to watch with his own eyes how his family would die. So he wanted to stay away for the time being.

It was well past noon and he was still not back. The kids had been pleading with their mother for the fish.

Now, his wife, who had been through a lot with him and loved him dearly, would never let the kids eat or taste anything before he had the first bite.

By the time the sun began to set in the west, the blowfish was still being cooked in the wok. It was then that he came back home, as if walking on air, dreading each step, his mind filled with pictures of his family, all dead, sprawled here and there.

Remembering his resolve to end the family's suffering, he quickened his steps. Even from a distance he could see the glistening eyes of his children waiting outside; then, he heard a chorus of their voices welcoming him home.

"Why, not dead yet?" he thought.

"Pop! We've been waiting for you to eat together!"

"Oh!" He knew now.

The family scrambled to the table and ate with gusto. They hadn't had any fish for so long and every tiny bite tasted delicious.

Afterwards, he lay in bed quietly and soon fell asleep, waiting for the Dark Angel of Death to descend.

The blowfish, however, had been cooked for so long its poison had all disappeared. So the family lived and would have to suffer hunger again, day by day.

He woke up and sighed: "Why is it so hard even to ask for death?" Tears welled from his eyes.

—Wang Renshu, from *The Pearl Jacket and Other Stories*

Pamelyn Casto

THE MYTH-ING LINK
(Or, Linking Up to Myth)

A Definition of Flash Fiction

Flash fiction is difficult if not impossible to define—and should be allowed to remain so—because this type of writing is protean. As with Proteus of ancient myth, it takes on various shapes and uses different strategies to achieve its goals. These shapes and strategies are too dissimilar to confine flash fiction to a too narrow or too specific definition. Flash fiction should not be fitted to a simple procrustean bed (the method used by mythical Procrustes; see prompt below). These short short stories are as endlessly metamorphosing as myths themselves. But I would tentatively define the best flash fiction as short short stories that manage to reveal the hidden, accentuate the subtle, and highlight the seemingly insignificant. Such stories allow readers, as William Blake said in another context, "to see a world in a grain of sand." The best offer insight and understanding of the human experience as they deepen and broaden reader awareness in a short space of text. While the stories as a whole often provide a quick flash of revelation, they are also read by serious readers as slowly and carefully as they might read good poetry. These highly charged stories often go well beyond their surface details and manage to expand in the reading.

Pamelyn Casto, raised in the Detroit area but now living in Texas, has hosted the popular FlashFiction-W critique group for over a decade. She is one of the few teachers of online courses in flash fiction and haibun (poetic prose pieces combined with haiku or tanka), and is editor of the free online *Flash Fiction Flash* monthly newsletter. Casto, who has been nominated for a Pushcart Prize, co-wrote numerous feature articles on writing flash fiction for *Writer's Digest* (and their other publications). She was commissioned to write an extensive article on flash fiction, which appears in *Books and Beyond: The Greenwood Encyclopedia of New American Reading* (4 volumes, 2008). She is co-editor (with Jessica Treat and Lawrence Greenberg) of a flash fiction anthology, tentatively titled *Freak Lightning*.

Notes on Flash Fiction from the Virtual Field

Due to my heavy involvement with flash fiction via the Internet, which is in many ways a modern-day labyrinth containing many hungry minotaurs, I have seen countless shapes and strategies for writing flash fiction. Flash fiction on the Net ranges from the simple, uncomplicated quick story—many times written by beginner writers to appeal to beginner editors—to highly complex and rich stories written by talented and experienced writers. In my active online flash fiction critique group, now ten years old and with a waiting list to join, the focus is on this type of writing only. We critique stories, discuss flash fiction writing theory, do story analyses, and write to story prompts. Thousands of stories from hundreds of writers have appeared on my computer screen over the years (some great and some that miss the mark).

Further, I teach fully interactive four-week courses in flash fiction. During the intense online courses that always fill to capacity (which seems to indicate a strong interest in flash fiction), participants read stories written by some of the best writers of flash fiction, analyze these stories, read articles and ideas on flash fiction, discuss writing theory, try various writing exercises, and critique resulting stories.

One popular and highly productive segment of the course is the study of, and writing from, myths. Participants read several old myths, mostly classical Greek, and then look at how modern flash fiction writers continue to make use of these enduring stories in a variety of ways. Some of the most interesting and memorable flash fiction written by those who take my course come out of the myth segment, and several participants have gone on to have their myth-inspired stories published as well.

Writers Working with Myth

Over time, many fine artists, poets, novelists, and short story writers have drawn upon myth for their work. A few of those writers are Eudora Welty, Sylvia Plath, Anne Sexton, John Barth, Christa Wolf, John Updike, Anne Carson, William Golding, Mary Renault, and C. S. Lewis. Recently (beginning in 2005), Canongate Books' Myth Series launched the first of its series of reimagined myths in short novel forms, a major and ambitious project involving many publishers and writers worldwide. A few of the writers involved in this project (who rewrote Greek myths) include Jeanette Winterson, Margaret Atwood, Victor Pelevin, David Grossman, Salley Vickers, and Michel Faber. Many more such novels in this series, including novels based on myths from around the world, are now or will be available in the near future. Myths obviously continue to intrigue writers and readers alike.

Many writers have also written outstanding flash fiction type pieces based on myth. Some of the best short short stories written by earlier writers (among many) include: "A Little Legend of the Dance" by Gottfried Keller (1819–90), "To Every Man His Chimera" by Charles Baudelaire (1821–67), and "Daedalus and Icarus" by Zbigniew Herbert (1924–98). Some contemporary writers who have written outstanding flash fiction using myth include: "Pygmalion" by John Updike, "Scheherazade" by Charles Baxter, "Silver Arrows" by Barry Yourgrau, and "Orion" by Jeanette Winterson. All these pieces are in the length range of flash fiction and all illustrate outstanding reuse of classical and well-known myths.

Re-Creation with Myths

Reworking myths allows writers to join in on the great conversations that have gone on through the ages. Through the study of mythology writers can also renew their own store of writing ideas. A good general mythology handbook or a Net search on classical myth can yield all sorts of myths begging to be reexamined and reshaped. Re-creating myths can be done in many ways, of course, and those ways are limited only by a writer's imagination and willingness to try something out of the ordinary. But two highly productive strategies involve showing how a myth is still alive today (through a type of literary shorthand or condensation) and reshaping stories by defamiliarizing older myths.

STRATEGY: Allow an Old Myth New Life
(Method of Literary Shorthand/Condensation)

"Myths are things that never happened, but always are." This statement from fourth-century Neoplatonic writer and philosopher Sallustius reminds modern writers that what is old can also take on new forms, can undergo new metamorphoses, can assume new transformations, and can generate new and interesting perspectives. Such stories represent the "is-ness of the was" (in the words of Russian religion and political philosopher Nicolai Berdyaev). Myths are never out of style, never lose their relevance—they merely metamorphose and serve different visions. Flash fiction writers can, to good effect, continue the long tradition of working with myths. These enduring stories can be freed from past confinement and undergo revisions, subversions, and transformations over and over again.

Ernest Hemingway compared an effective story to an iceberg, where the largest percentage of the iceberg is submerged beneath the surface. Drawing upon characters or archetypes from mythology provides a way of making use of underlying stories—an effective literary shorthand method of telling a story, a way of condensing or compressing a modern story by drawing upon an older story. This strategy can aid in creating good and expandable flash fiction since the older myth would also be at work beneath the surface details.

For instance, merely through the use of an appropriate name from myth, in a character's name or in a story's title, a writer can imply an iceberg of information without having to actually provide that information. In his short short story "Pygmalion," John Updike did not have to tell readers that this story involves a man who tries to create the ideal woman. Instead, Updike shows us how this well-known archetype from myth continues his pattern into modern times. In Charles Baxter's "Sheherazade," Baxter names the myth character in his title and shows her living in modern times and involved in a modern situation (and he also gives the traditional story an interesting twist). Through Baxter's story, Sheherazade continues telling stories to prolong a life. Names drawn from myth, used in a character's name or a story title, can be a way to deepen a story, as when the part stands for the whole or the whole stands for the part, and which draws upon or is supported by a story or stories that came before—as the larger part of the iceberg beneath the surface details.

STRATEGY: Defamiliarization

Karen Armstrong, in her book *A Short History of Myth*, which serves as the introduction to the recent Canongate Books' series of myths in novel form, says, "Like science and technology, mythology . . . is not about opting out of this world, but about enabling us to live more intensely within it." Writers who study and become aware of the many myths that continue to inform our lives can create even more interesting and meaningful stories by drawing upon this rich store of writing possibilities.

Defamiliarization, a concept developed by formalist Viktor Shklovsky in his *Art as Technique*, is a productive strategy for creating memorable flash fiction from myths. Shklovksy says, "The technique of art is to make objects 'unfamiliar,' to make forms difficult, to increase the difficulty and length of perception because the process of perception is an aesthetic end in itself and must be prolonged."

The process of defamiliarization of a familiar myth disturbs readers' normal perceptions and understandings and encourages them to read more attentively and carefully. Making the familiar unfamiliar helps renew perception and aids in breaking the deadening habit of easy interpretation and assumptions. A defamiliarized myth will not meet readers' usual expectations and consequently pushes readers to see things as if they were new. It allows readers to perceive the myth or the specific situation in a new light and they are then put in the position of living/reading more intensely—since their previous knowledge is called into question and they are outside their safely familiar assumptions and understandings. Such a strategy disturbs comfortable knowledge, unsettles usual perceptions, and of necessity prolongs reader contemplation. Such stories allow a reader and writer to live more intensely within the newly written defamiliarized myth.

Robert Hill Long's story (p. 30) serves as an outstanding example of a writer drawing upon a familiar myth to create a new metamorphosis through the method of defamiliarization. The usual or common understanding of the myth of the Sphinx is that she destroyed herself when Oedipus answered her riddle. But Long subverts the known myth, makes it counter common knowledge and understanding, and achieves a new transformation of the myth. Long's defamiliarized Sphinx continues to present her riddle to readers (in a three-part piece). As a result, the story makes a fascinating addition to the endlessly mutating, forever metamorphosing forms of myth.

This story—and those you can create from the prompts below—will allow you to rethink familiar myths, to see them in new ways, and will lead to the discovery of new possibilities for your own flash fiction.

~*~

A FLASH FICTION PROMPT

To begin metamorphosing myths, get a good general mythology handbook to aid you. My preference is *The Meridian Handbook of Classical Mythology* by Edward Tripp (1970) because it contains so much source material. Or you can do a Net search for classical Greek myth. Then take any well-known mythic character and show how the archetype continues to live in the modern world. Or take any well-known myth and defamiliarize it. Below are some starter possibilities you might consider.

1. Echo cannot initiate conversation but is doomed to repeat the words of others. What sort of modern-day job might she have? What if she accidentally said something original?

2. In two different traditions, Pandora and Eve are the "first woman" created. Try a Q&A–type story in which the two are interviewed or put on trial.

3. Adephagia is the goddess of gluttony. What form might her self-indulgent excesses take today?

4. Procrustes is known for his odd habits as a host. When he had visitors who did not fit in his guest bed, he either stretched them or lopped off their extremities to make them fit. Maybe set his story in a modern hotel, motel, or bed-and-breakfast.

5. The Graeae are two old, white-haired women who had only one eye and one tooth between them, and Perseus stole even these. Try putting them in a nursing home where they tell their story—their way.

6. Priapus is a fertility god who possesses enormous genitals. He got into a bragging contest with a talking ass over who had the larger size. Priapus lost. (A modern note: one of the side effects of

certain modern male enhancement drugs is a condition known as priapism—named for Priapus.)

7. Hestia, one of the Olympians, remained a virgin and chose not to marry. She tends the home fires of her parents, Cronus and Rhea. Could she also represent a victim of agoraphobia?

A STORY EXAMPLE

The Sphinx

It is not true that the heroes died because the sphinx was terrifying to behold or her riddle too hard. When one sauntered up, full of youth bravado, she put away her knitting needles, folded the wings behind her back and asked in a demure voice where he had been so long and whether he wanted anything to drink. At the sight of milk dripping from her full breasts, he fell into a speechless baby-gurgle and in a day or two died of thirst at her feet. Oedipus already knew whom he was going to marry: he simply wanted lion-claws and eagle-wings to impress her.

Nor is it true that the sphinx killed herself because Oedipus used her to perfect his habit of drop-dead retorts to every question. Yes, his indifference to what she might do afterward, the way he averted his eyes when he answered, these things infuriated her. But not even a myth of guilt existed yet: destroying herself before his eyes would have been pointless. Instead she assumed the formlessness of the horizon. From this vantage point she could survey the whole course of Greek tragedy degenerating into barbaric romances, situation comedies, thirty-second ads for hair replenisher.

She is still there, shawled in heat-shimmer or in a cold drizzle. Though her milk dried up centuries ago, it still gives her pleasure to watch the tiny hordes of question marks trying to approach her, like tourists. At sunset it is possible to imagine her faint, flushed smile as she savors the moment Oedipus raises the familiar knitting needles and plunges them into his eyes.

—Robert Hill Long

Tom Hazuka

FLASH FICTION FROM EMBRYO TO (VERY SHORT) ADULT

As one of the editors of the original *Flash Fiction* anthology, you'd think that I could remember who came up with that catchy title. I say "catchy" because obviously the term has caught on: Google that alliterative pair of words "flash fiction" and you'll find something in the neighborhood of 1,210,000 references. Even recourse to my journal from 1988, the year we began our research for the book, provides no definitive answers. Believe me, I was hoping for an entry that proved the title was my idea. As much as I'd love to take credit, though, my best guess is that "flash fiction" was the brainchild of my co-editor James Thomas. I'll just take a small pat on the back for supporting that title, not vetoing it.

Before *Flash Fiction*, I had helped James Thomas and Robbie Shapard edit *Sudden Fiction* and *Sudden Fiction International*, and every year I'd send an entry to the *Sun Dog* World's Best Short Short Story Competition at Florida State. Those two experiences set my personal mental framework for short short stories: about 1,500 words max for sudden fiction, 250 words max for the contest (a length that later came to be known as micro fiction). *Flash Fiction* staked out a middle ground of around 750 words, a number we did not arrive at without plenty of discussion. Over time, the flash fiction definition has expanded depending on who's doing

Tom Hazuka is co-editor of the popular W. W. Norton *Flash Fiction* anthology (1992), with James and Denise Thomas. With Mark Budman (p. 125), he co-edited *Best American Flash Fiction of the 21st Century* (Shanghai Foreign Language Education Press, 2007) and the prize-winning *You Have Time for This: Contemporary American Short-Short Stories* (2007). Hazuka, recipient of the Bruce P. Rossley Award for New England Writers, has published three novels, including *In the City of the Disappeared* (2000). Raised in Westbrook, Connecticut, he spent 15 years mostly out of state in California, Utah, and Chile. He returned to Connecticut in 1992 to teach at Central Connecticut State University, and is currently writing a memoir of his time in Chile under the Pinochet dictatorship.

the deciding, and that's fine. A little elasticity can be a good thing. For example, in our 2007 flash fiction anthology *You Have Time for This*, Mark Budman and I set a limit of 500 words, while Rose Metal Press uses a ceiling of 1,000. To my mind, stories longer than 1,000 words edge out of flash fiction territory and into the realm of sudden fiction.

When *Flash Fiction* was published in 1992, we heard querulous comments about the book being pabulum for the attenuated attention span of the MTV generation. Such complaints are almost nonexistent today, despite ubiquitous video games, myriad TV channels, and turbo-charged remote controls. Flash fiction has since established itself as a respectable genre, both because much of it is good literature, and because many well-known, top-shelf authors are writing it. If an art form is good enough for John Updike, Joyce Carol Oates, Stuart Dybek, Francine Prose, Raymond Carver, Tim O'Brien, Jamaica Kincaid, and Margaret Atwood (to name just a few of the writers in *Flash Fiction*), it's tough to dismiss as "fiction lite," or some other disparaging term.

My response to denigrators of flash fiction has always been simple: if you think it's so easy to write, I dare you to give it a try. My students are consistently surprised to learn that for most of them, flash fiction is far harder to write than a longer piece. Making a story happen, and especially making a story *work* in such a condensed space, is a huge challenge. (I'm reminded of Mark Twain's apology for writing a long letter, saying he didn't have time to write a short one.) As in a poem, every word needs to matter, but there's the additional requirement of narrative. No one condemns a poem as dunce-fodder if it's short. Why should fiction be held to a different standard, an artificial and arbitrary one at that?

One cool thing about flash fiction is that it's nearly impossible to be formulaic when writing a successful piece of contemporary flash. The shorter the story, the tougher it is to copy well-worn patterns. Genre conventions need space to play out in their predictable ways. Flash fiction tends to require invention and imagination in its execution. You can't rely on mimicking what's been done before in order to write your way out of a story.

Flash fiction is dear to me not only because *Flash Fiction* was the first book with my name on the cover. It also steered me in a direction that became my first novel, *The Road to the Island*. After three years of editing *Flash Fiction*, and reading some 5,000 flash pieces, I hit upon what I thought was a brilliant idea: write a novel whose chapters are each a flash fiction story that can be read on its own, independently of the book. The plan soon proved to be unworkable, at least for my ability, but flash fiction was the catalyst I needed to get started. And for that I am forever grateful.

Studies and statistics say that Americans are reading less and less. Partially that's because people are lazy and prefer *American Idol*, but it's also because they are horribly busy and have little time for reading. With flash fiction, though, no matter how busy you are, literature can be part of your day. If nothing else, keep a flash book in the bathroom. (I semi-seriously joke that *Flash Fiction* would be a bestseller if retitled *Flush Fiction* and marketed as the ultimate bathroom companion.) If you are reading this now you are either a fan of flash fiction or willing to give it a chance, and I wish you well. At the very least, *You Have Time for This*.

✒

A FLASH FICTION EXERCISE

Point of view and voice are crucial to all fiction, but especially with flash fiction, when so much needs to be told and shown within a short space. If you're having trouble with a flash piece, experiment with a different point of view and/or a different context for the "same" events. Most of my flash fiction is in first person. The shorter the story, the more likely it is that I use first person, because the voice of an "I" creates efficient double-duty characterization. Anything the narrator says not only provides information, it also shows who that narrator is; it's not just what you say, it's how you say it. One character at a ball game might be engrossed in the action, while the person at his side might be bored and more interested in finding a beer vendor. These characters are at the same event, but each would give the reader a vastly different view of what's happening.

Changing a detail or two can greatly affect your story. For example, the tone of a sports spectator would vary depending on whether his team is winning or losing, whether he has a large bet riding on the outcome, whether that jerk sitting next to him would shut up and watch the game instead of screaming for the beer vendor, and so on. The "same" person would have a different perspective at 16 years old than at 50. Attending the game with your parents is one thing, with your children quite another—and with your parents *and* your children yet another.

For practice, change some details in my story "Utilitarianism" to create a different experience for the reader. "The Tet Offensive" or "Operation Desert Storm" would establish a more recent historical setting than "Guadalcanal," for example. In particular, try to imagine the story from the point of view of one or both of the parents.

A STORY EXAMPLE

Utilitarianism

I return home for the first time as an adult. My parents greet me traditionally, Mom worrying "that woman" isn't feeding me enough, Dad crushing my hand lest I forget which one of us survived Guadalcanal. But an odor of arrested decay has replaced the smells of childhood. The house of my youth is decorated with death.

Stuffed creatures fill the rooms. Local varmints predominate— squirrels, chipmunks, some possums and porcupines, even a bullfrog—but Dad hangs my coat on an eight-point buck, and the TV blares from the belly of a rampant and silently roaring grizzly. We stand entranced, almost touching.

"I bet you could eat a horse," Mom says, and bustles to the kitchen.

"You know Jeremy Bentham, the philosopher?" Dad asks. "*He's* stuffed. Mom and I are going to London to see him."

My father has hardly left the state since World War II.

"Your favorite! Liverwurst on rye."

Mom puts the sandwich and a glass of milk on the dining room table. Then I see that the cat I grew up with is the centerpiece.

"You embalmed Kitten!"

"Embalming is for graveyards, son. Mom and I fixed Kitten to be with us forever."

I can't eat with a corpse staring at me. "Where did you get all these, these *dead* things?"

"My God, boy," Mom says. "Open your eyes." A shadow nicks her face. "I thought you loved liverwurst."

"Your mother saw the ad in the magazine," Dad says, the two of them beaming as he puts his arm around her for the first time in my memory.

—Tom Hazuka, from *Quarterly West*

Jayne Anne Phillips

"CHEERS," (or) HOW I TAUGHT MYSELF TO WRITE

In the late seventies, when I began writing them, I called them "one-page fictions." I don't really like the term "flash fictions"; there's nothing flashy or spangled or shiny (superficial) about a great one-page fiction. The successful one-page fiction is a whole story in a paragraph or three: just as strong, tensile, and whole as the well-written story, novella, novel. The great one-page fiction is intensely compressed, every line weighted precisely, every image firing on multiple levels. Good one-page fictions have a spiral construction: the words circle out from a dense, packed core, and the spiral moves through the words, past the boundary of the page. That limitless quality could be said to apply to great fiction of any length, but the realized one-page fiction must move palpably beyond the page, like a ghost self. The words of the last line should create a silence, a white space in which the reader breathes. The story enters that breath, and continues.

I didn't realize it at the time, but I taught myself to write by writing one-page fictions. I found in the form the density I needed, the attention to the line, the syllable. I began writing as a poet. In the one-page form, I found the freedom of the paragraph. I learned to understand

Born and raised in West Virginia, *Jayne Anne Phillips* is the author of four novels, *Lark and Termite* (2009), *Motherkind* (2000), *Shelter* (1994), and *Machine Dreams* (1984), and two collections of stories: *Fast Lanes* (1987) and *Black Tickets* (1979). Published when she was just 26 and described by Raymond Carver as "stories unlike any in our literature," the latter collection foreshadowed the resurgence of the flash form by interspersing her one-page fictions from *Sweethearts* (1976) among longer stories to create an "imagistic, novelistic arc." Winner of a Guggenheim Fellowship, two National Endowment for the Arts Fellowships, a Bunting Fellowship, a National Book Critics Circle Award nomination, and an Orange Prize nomination, Phillips is currently professor of English and director of the MFA Program at Rutgers–Newark, in New Jersey.

the paragraph as secretive and subversive. The poem in broken lines announces itself as a poem, but the paragraph seems innocent, workaday, invisible. The paragraph is simply the form of written information: instruction booklets, tax forms, newspapers, cookbooks: all are written in paragraphs. We read the lines; the words enter us. The poem inside the paragraph is a mainlined image: it shoots right into the vein, into the blood, so to speak, of meaning, and the reader takes it in before arming himself or herself against it.

I use literature itself as a prompt in the teaching of writing, and I often ask students to write one-page fictions: the form demands economy, precision, and the attention to every word that is necessary in each line we write. The form demands a great title, a title that is redefined by the story, and attains more layers of meaning, each time we read the story. One-page fictions demand an individual lyricism, a musical sound, a rhythm and stress in each phrase. The form demands an end line that is conclusive, perfect, powerful, and moves beyond the page (see above). One-page fictions should not be throwaways just because they're short; they should not be flippant or merely clever. They should tell real stories that are lean and strong in one paragraph, or two, or three. I typically give students my own compendium of examples, a self-selected (changing) textbook of favorite one-page fictions by various authors, and let them see what they are inspired to write. Language is associative, I remind my students. Let us associate with language: one word leads to the next, and images build organically, in sync, if we listen to what we're writing.

My own first chapbook was a collection of twenty-four one-page fictions. The cover image was my parents' wedding picture, and one of the fictions included is called "Wedding Picture." It's the story of a marriage in three paragraphs, told in images, based on an image: a description of a photograph informed by the writer's knowledge of past, present, and future beyond the photograph. I show students the cover of the chapbook and invite them to write a one-page fiction about their own parents' wedding picture. They bring the pictures to class when they share the work; we sometimes compose a book of wedding pictures and their stories. Students have written about their adoptive parents' wedding pictures, or written about the empty space in which their parents' wedding picture does not exist. One student wrote about the orphanage in which he'd spent most of his childhood and supplied a photograph of the orphanage. We talk about real life, and the fact that literature, like a photograph, begins, somehow, in what is real, and transforms what happened into what it means—a living meaning no longer bound by the limitations of time, space, or fact. I suppose it's no accident that the "subtitle" of the MFA program I designed at Rutgers–Newark is "Real Lives, Real Stories." I don't think we can tell real stories, fiction that creates a reality, unless we lead real lives: for the writer, the real life is the life that finds meaning in literature: in reading literature, learning literature, being guided, taught, wounded, supported, beckoned forward, by literature. Literature can teach us how to live before we live, and how to die before we die. I believe that writing is practice for death, and for every (other) transformation human beings encounter. Writing is alchemy. The one-page fiction can be a compressed, weighted, perfectly balanced, read-in-one-moment example of the miracle. Fast, precise, over. And not over. The one-page fiction should hang in the air of the mind like an image made of smoke.

A FLASH FICTION PROMPT

Write a one-page fiction about your parents' or guardians' wedding picture, and bring the picture to class with copies of your fiction. You know a history the photograph does not, and the photograph "knows" a moment you did not experience. If your parents or guardians never married, imagine the photograph that might have existed if they had, or work with a photograph of them that most clearly defines a pivotal moment in their relationship. Use the physical details of the photograph to move into the story. Don't tell the story; suggest it within the language.

A STORY EXAMPLE

Wedding Picture

My mother's ankles curve from the hem of a white suit as if the bones were water. Under the cloth her body in its olive skin unfolds.

Russell Randolph Phillips and Martha Jane Thornhill, May 1948.
Used by permission of Jayne Anne Phillips.

The black hair, the porcelain neck, the red mouth that barely shows its teeth. My mother's eyes are round and wide as a light behind her skin burns them to coals. Her heart makes a sound that no one hears. The sound says each fetus floats, an island in the womb.

My father stands beside her in his brown suit and two-tone shoes. He stands also by the plane in New Guinea in 1944. On its side there is a girl on a swing wearing spike heels and short shorts. Her breasts balloon; the sky opens inside them. Yellow hair smooth as cats, she is swinging out to him. He glimmers, blinded by the light. Now his big fingers curl inward. He is trying to hold something.

In her hands the snowy Bible hums, nuns swarming a honeyed cell. The husband is an afterthought. Five years since the high school lover crumpled on the bathroom floor, his sweet heart raw. She's twenty-three, her mother's sick, it's time. My father's heart pounds, a bell in a wrestler's chest. He is almost forty and the lilies are trumpeting. Rising from his shoulders, the cross grows pale and loses its arms in their heads.

—Jayne Anne Phillips, from *Sweethearts*

Stuart Dybek

GREAT THOUGHTS

In Richard Brautigan's story collection *Revenge of the Lawn,* there's a four-sentence piece titled "Lint" that I often bring to writing workshops. Sometimes I also bring on the first day of class the gift of a pocket notebook for each student. It isn't to be used as a journal, but as a Great Thoughts Notebook. I think of it as akin to the sketchbook that artists carry—that pad of paper by which the hand through exercise acquires its own intelligence. A notebook is a net for collecting stray perceptions, dreams, which are usually only the fragments of dreams, memories, which are usually only the fragments of events, and other fragments: images, lines of dialogue, quotations from books—stuff that Brautigan might call lint, which opens with the narrator feeling haunted by emotions he is unable to capture in words and by events he can only explain in those *dimensions of lint.*

I wonder what Brautigan himself thought his piece titled "Lint" was. He wrote poems as well as stories, but he includes "Lint" with his story collection published by Simon and Schuster in 1971, sixteen years before the seminal anthology *Sudden Fiction* appeared and gave the short short prose form the identity that comes with a flashy name.

I've been examining half-scraps of my childhood. They are pieces of

Stuart Dybek was born and raised on Chicago's South Side, where much of his writing is set. An MFA graduate from the University of Iowa, Dybek's numerous awards include a Whiting Writers Award, multiple O. Henry awards, and a MacArthur Fellowship. His short short prose has been collected into the highly acclaimed *Brass Knuckles* (1979) and *The Coast of Chicago* (1990). In 2008, a French translation and expansion of his 1993 chapbook of shorts *The Story of Mist* was published by Siloe in Paris. Known for his strong narrative voice, his lyricism, and his vivid, almost folkloric memories of childhood, many critics consider him one of our foremost writers of flash fiction. He is currently distinguished writer in residence at Northwestern University and a faculty member of Western Michigan University's Prague Summer Program.

distant life that have no form or meaning. They are things that just hap-pened like lint.

Most writers I know keep a notebook. I've kept one since college. I write things down not simply to save them, but to practice writing, to connect perception and language so as to make them indistinguishable from one another. I've lost a few of those notebooks over the years, but there's one especially whose loss I mourn. After college I worked as a caseworker in Chicago. My district was on the South Side, not far from where I was raised. I was living on the North Side and on the L ride across the city, to and from work, I'd scribble in my notebook. It had a soft, slick, brown cover, and fit comfortably in my back pocket. I wish I could find a notebook like that to buy today. I meant to record the scenes of street life I saw in those disadvantaged neighborhoods, but the rhythm of the train carried me back to growing up in my own neighborhood, and I began sketching those recollections, or in Brautigan's words, "examining half-scraps of my childhood." Those scraps were indeed without "form or meaning"—an air shaft, I remembered, that my bedroom window opened on, and the vague outlines of fallen things that lay three stories down at the bottom of it. The gray smell of its shadowy light. There weren't stories that went with these recollections, but they were not without sentiment. I wrote to see if I could remake the memory on the page, and feeling appeared like a byproduct. In creation myths, a god shapes mud or clay into living form, much like a potter throws a pot or a sculptor reveals the statue within a block of marble. But a writer has to create his own clay or stone before he can begin shaping life from it. I hoped that if I wrote enough such scraps, they might connect into a whole, that is, into a shape I recognized from reading, the shape of a story or a poem. W. H. Auden, who was a great keeper of notebooks, described a poem as being written by connecting the best lines from a notebook.

The gift that the notebook I kept on those L rides gave me, however, was not the gift of wholes, but a permission to lose myself in the making of fragments. Rather than recognizing what the connections were that made for recognizable forms, there was the recognition that the fragments themselves conveyed feeling—something not unlike what Poe called effect. For Poe, a story did not have to end in a moral or with a plot neatly tied up in a bow. We remember certain details—scraps, lint—because they are connected to feeling, and to recreate them on the page so that the reader too experiences the feeling is an effect.

Now that, other than lint, there's a name, or rather, names, for them—flash fiction, sudden fiction, microfiction, the short short, fragments as they're called in France—they're easier to recognize. They've become a genre, with a history, and models, and one can sit down and conceive of a piece of flash fiction from scratch, rather than finding it in one's back pages, already written as if by accident.

I lost that notebook on a grand drunken night, either at the taco joint called El Serape, or later at the jazz club where John Coltrane was playing. The next morning I retraced my steps, trying to find it. I never managed to recreate those lost pieces written on the L, but I continued recording scraps. Some did connect and shape themselves into stories and poems. Others remained fragments with their byproduct of feeling, and some of those I sorted out, reframed on the white space of a page, and tinkered with until their incompleteness seemed somehow just complete enough.

⌒ff⌒

A FLASH FICTION PROMPT

Keep a Great Thoughts Notebook for at least a week. Try to recall the "lint" from your childhood, then pick one scrap of memory that will build on itself to convey the most feeling. Reframe your memory so that it has the form of a story—start with an opening description, then shift gear to a second character and dialogue. For me, this shift is what turns it into a story. For the closure, one of my favorite ways to end is with a final line of dialogue, as in Hemingway's *The Sun Also Rises:* "Isn't it pretty to think so?"

A STORY EXAMPLE

Confession

Father Boguslaw was the priest I waited for, the one whose breath through the thin partition of the confessional reminded me of the ventilator behind Vic's Tap. He huffed and smacked as if in response to my dull litany of sins, and I pictured him slouched in his cubicle, draped in vestments, the way he sat slumped in the back entrance to the sacristy before saying morning mass—hung over, sucking an unlit Pall Mall, exhaling smoke.

Once, his head thudded against the wooden box.

"Father," I whispered, "Father," but he was out, snoring. I knelt, wondering what to do, until he finally groaned and hacked himself awake.

As usual, I'd saved the deadly sins for last: the lies and copied homework, snitching drinks, ditching school, hitchhiking, which I'd been convinced was an offense against the Fifth Commandment, which prohibited suicide. Before I reached the dirty snapshots of Korean girls, stolen from the dresser of my war hero uncle, Uncle Al, and still unrepentantly cached behind the oil shed, he knocked and said I was forgiven.

As for Penance: "Go in peace, my son, I'm suffering enough today for both of us."

—Stuart Dybek, from *The Story of Mist*

Michael Martone

TITLED: THE TITLE
A Short Short Story's Own Short Short Story

I write long, long titles for my short, short stories. I suppose this is, for me, existential, a function of the genre, a genre that defines itself, first, with this intensified brevity—the *short* short. But what kind of brevity? What is the quality of "brief"? The shortness of the short, the short shortness has, most often, to do with word count and, also (though less often) with the word count's relationship with page length and, by extension, the number of pages. I have noticed that the genre's most definite defining instruction found in the guidelines for contest and anthology solicitations spells out the length of "short." It seems length is, perhaps, our only agreed upon convention. Adrift, in the miasmic nebulousness of this form, it is comforting to count beans, to have beans to count on. The prompt to write this something we call the short short story is addressed in terms of numbers of words—250, 500, 1,000—or numbers of pages— one page or complete on two facing pages. Often, the only defining characteristic of the short short story is this kind of length, or lack thereof. At the very least, length as a defining characteristic goes a long way, a kind of essential DNA, as close as we get to formula or rules.

I believe this piece here was to measure out at 2,000 words (or so I

Born and raised in Fort Wayne, Indiana, *Michael Martone* earned an English degree from Indiana University and graduated from The Writing Seminars at Johns Hopkins. Considered by many to be one of the most influential practitioners of the contemporary American short short, his many published works range from short story and essay collections, to articles, reviews, and even a "travel guide." Widely anthologized, his fiction appears in *Flash Fiction* (1992), *Sudden Fiction* (1996), and W. W. Norton's *Micro Fiction* (1996), and he is co-editor with Lex Williford (p. 76) of two anthologies. Known for his emphasis on place, his essay collection *The Flatness and Other Landscapes* (2000), about the Midwest, won the AWP Prize for Creative Nonfiction. He teaches and has directed the creative writing program at the University of Alabama.

remember).[1] Yes, 2,000 words. But let me burn some of those words on this aside. Just how quaint, how antique to use that particular scale of numbers—250, 500, 1,000—numbered by such metrics for this genre of short fiction, already strange because the genre is already mostly characterized by word count, page count, but so curious also that the word count, page count is still based on the ancient typewritten page of 250 words. This makes me think that the form, perhaps, is a creature, most of all, not of the handwritten page but of the typewritten page or of the computer written page—the computer hobbled to act like the antiquated nineteenth-century machine. I am at this moment using double-spaced Courier on my iMac to mimic the typewriter and the 250-word page. All of this to say that this is a lot of words to say this: if an essential part of the form is the formal limitation of words, and if every word counts in the form, then do the number of words in the title count in the count?

I like to think when I think about word count, that the words floating at the top of this column in the header don't count. That the words in the title inhabit a kind of duty-free zone of existence, the realm of untaxed perfume and spirits, a transient space unencumbered where one passes through, where one is nowhere and everywhere. The title is like the hidden text of the computer page, that 50%-gray ghost print. The title, like the fields of headers and footers, is para-text, graying in the gray area, so when whatever editorial assistant sits down to count the words to see if this or that piece is the right kind of short to be a short short story, he or she will start with the "I" with which this essay started and regard the title starting with "Titled" as a kind of gimme, a practice swing, a tune up, a fumbling-focus, throat-clearing, tuning-fork tabulation that it is and it isn't. Now, the computer is not so forgiving. This word here, this "here" is word 603 according to the meter running at the bottom of the frame of this open window and embedded in that number 603 are the 11 words of the title. I have used over 603 words, one way or another, to get to this point, right here, all to say only that titles, whether they count or not in the accountancy of word count rules, count. And because we most often

---

[1] But I should go back and look at the original correspondence.

take titles for granted—they're granted to us—we don't grant to them much of the much more they could be.

Where is it written that we as writers need to title what we write? It is a convention so deeply ingrained as to be invisible to us. The practice, no doubt, reaches back to some primordial primary grade school lesson of composition writing by rote. "Now class, begin your paper with a 'title' and remember to center your title on the first line. . . ." Yes, there are the experiments of avoiding the imperative of the title, such as titling the title "Untitled" or titling with cardinal or ordinal numbers that now can incorporate the digital dot to the various versions—Title 2.0—to the numeric sequence. Yes, the generic "Poem" and the more rare "Story" or "A Story" have been used but they are still titles even as they resist title-ness, and yes, even the Dickinsonian blankness that is left blank gets filled by the default of the first line that follows the purposeful nothingness. The text abhors this vacuum. Tide and title rush in.

For the prose writer, the title is as close as he or she will get to writing a poem. The poem loves to play close, in the valence of individual words and their multiple meanings, sometime contradictory, meanings the words embody as well as the lubricated surfaces of several such words rubbing up against one another. The example I love is from W. H. Auden and his partial line:[2]

Poetry makes nothing happen…

The pressure is all over the word "nothing" and the simultaneity of its making "makes nothing happen" and "nothing happening" a force forcing the reader to inflect with personal emphasis the English spin on this particular cue. The poem can have us, has had us, read (at least) both ways of reading at the same time, as well as sequentially backward and forward, the exact inexactness of the sense. A poem and a title, I am arguing here, fight against the existential nature of the medium of prose that insists the words line up, be read in order and with a syntax that yanks the kinks out of convolution. A poem and in this case a title want to be inhaled all at once, a fast-acting pill dissolving. Like a painting, poetry

---

[2] Which would make a great title, by the way.

is a wall of sense and senselessness that is at once centered and in the periphery. The title, this kind of poem, then does not so much participate in the stylistic ideal of the prose it precedes. It is not interested in transparency, a clear window transmission of the content. Instead, the title hedges. It is a thicket, a bramble, a roll of concertina wire. It contains one thing and at least one thing more, and it contains the one thing and all of the everythings the piece the title titles is not. The story is a maze one works one's way through. The title is the maze's maze.

The picture postcard's stamp is the picture postcard's picture postcard. Stamps are highly elaborated works of art[3] we routinely carry around, often overlooked as our attention is focused upon the thing "underneath," the scribbled greeting or the view out the vacation window. The title too is frank franking, a stamp to validate and to cancel. It shares space and time with the card; its affixing in fact animates the card, the last piece, a kind of key that propels it through the world. But at the same time both the stamp and the title remain aloof, separate from the things they attach to and with their own aesthetic. The title and the stamp are both symbiotic and autonomic. Their vision is both binocular and depthless, a gem seen through a jeweler's loupe.

A long title at the beginning of a very short story alerts in a reader's mind not so much the meaning, theme, or content of the prose but the slant notion of scale itself. A short short story may be about a lot of things but one thing it is always about is scale. It is about the strategy of concentration, compaction, compression, as if the prose were being squeezed by some piston to the point of spontaneous combustion. The title then works to machine this shrinkage. You work through the title like a sieve, a filter. Negotiating a title recalibrates you to this new world you are about to enter, no longer metered in meters but now in microns or angstroms. The title acclimates you through its distortions to the distortions to come, a zoom lens attached to the microscope.

How small is small finally? An element, say, or the atoms inside the elements or the nucleus and electron shells inside the atom, the particles inside the protons and electrons, the particles of particles, the small

---

[3] As is currency, both paper and coin.

that is finally undetectable. How long is a short short story? How short is it to be? How long is the title, this other entity that orbits the thing it titles? Is it a satellite, a moon, a belt of dust? Or can the title be a collapsed star, dense and deep, that the story in its flight is hinged upon? The title perhaps is the still center that snaps the story around; indeed, the story must be read in full to finally unlock the meaning of the title. The title's not a simple introduction at all but the question posed for the story to answer. Perhaps the short short story we really write is the title. And the short short story we do write, that falls in letters from the title down the page like a curtain or a matrix of stars, is nothing more than an overlarge enabling apparatus for the few words of the title. As a writer of the short short story my desire is, by definition, to be as short as possible, short squared. So what can be shorter than a title?

The short short story's short short story. That next step toward the shortness that in its even less-ness is next to Godliness.

✍

A FLASH FICTION EXERCISE

Title Everything

Write a story. Double-space. Now make each sentence a stand alone. Title each sentence. As if each were a story. Fifty sentences. Fifty titles to the 50 sentences. In the end, collect the titles. Arrange them as if they were a story. A story made up of 50 sentences.

Or

In Which You Gloss

Write a story. Or take one of the stories you have already written. Gloss it in the manner of old novel chapters. *In which our Pip discovers he has a benefactor,* etc. Be sure that the gloss touches all the salient plot points, reveals the action of the piece, its moral. Use the gloss now as the title of the piece. Go back to the story and cut all the sentences dealing with the material now contained in the gloss.

Or finally

Simply

Write a story in which the title is longer than the story. Experiment with that. And then write a story in collage fragments, each of which is titled with a title longer than the piece it titles.

A STORY EXAMPLE

A Perimenopausal Jacqueline Kennedy, Two Years After the Assassination, Aboard the M/Y *Christina*, off Eubeoa, Bound for the Island of Alonnisos, Devastated by a Recent Earthquake, Drinks Her Fourth Bloody Mary with Mrs. Franklin Delano Roosevelt, Jr.

The barstools' seats are covered with the foreskins of whales, Ari loves to tell his guests, and it was at this bar that Jack first met Mr. Churchill, but you know that, you've heard that before, as I am in the habit of wading through the historic, an archipelago of scattered captions, a sign myself, I allocute, droning through the landscape of vetted plaque language, appositives and modifiers and subordinate and restrictive clauses, the constellations of museum labels, your taped tour guide, who sooner-or-later says the barstools of the *Christina* were upholstered with the foreskins of whales, *baleen,* and on them Jack who would be President sat drinking Bloody Marys with the former wartime Prime Minister of that precious stone set in a silver sea, that other Eden, that England, two sailors they fancied themselves, their fannies parked on the tooled foreskins of whales, *cetacean.*

o

The right whale got its name for being the right whale to kill, and off the Vineyard we chased the whalers chasing a panicked pod sounding and sliding down beneath the launch like sleek needles sliding beneath skin. The cows are each as big as islands and sleep like reefs, lolling, the rookery of birds along the rocky spine starting every time a calf breaches, leaping up on a mother's back, slipping off and into the water and breaching again and tumbling back, again and again, trying to wake her, it could be days, a wake of waking.

o

The *Christina* is itself a big white whale making way with its trailing catalogue of chase boats though this flotilla appears thinned, anemic compared to when we cruised off Ithaca after Patrick died, remember? They thought they caught me then, broadsides of tele-photo lenses. Now they lag. They stall. Chips off the ship, it seems, they grow smaller in the distance, wreaths or buoys, wallowing in the troughs of waves, our own towed islet chain, a random map.

o

Cyclades, Dodecanese, Ionian, Sporades—the island chains. Skíros, Skópelos, Alónnisos, Skíathos are the Sporades we are steaming to, we are steaming to the Sporades, sporadic in the northern Aegean. Spores. You should see the charts. Someone has cast the joints of bone like dice, not so much a chain, these islands, but a broken and scattered string of phalanges, and now the dice-like houses on those dice-like islands have tumbled down the dice-like chockablock ba-salt acropoli, the *Hora* horribly tossed and tossed into the agitated sea, new peninsulas of chunky ruin, deltas of limey whitewashed dust. Ari says we will all give blood, our blue, blue blood when we get there. The *Christina*'s hold holds vats of water, pallets of blan-kets, bushel bags of sour *trahanas,* and egg-crates of bottled gas—a dry goods convoy to another powdered and pulverized disaster.

o

I always heard it said that George Jessel invented the Bloody Mary, half vodka and half tomato juice, the after-drinks drink, a sober drink to get you drunk the first thing after the last thing you remem-ber, the transfused eulogy. All the blood in the world could not save Patrick who died drowning in the liquefied air in which his lungs came packed like a surplus jeep in cosmolene. He was early. It is late. We island hopped too through that mourning. One tragedy after another. The syrup of tomato is just what the doctor ordered, an elixir, a tincture, a kind of plasma. To my blue baby. To the Toast-master General, our contemporary Pericles who works blue.

o

To avoid the circling bulls, the she whale rolls over on her back, and it's a sight to see to see the males attempt to mate that way, climbing, scooting up the beach with all that now not buoyant tonnage, up over her underbelly to the peak of the breach of her and her, just then, rolling over to take a breath before she rolls back over again on her back—a shoal, a hostile jetty, an unnavigable bar. This too goes on for hours, for days as everything with whales runs in whale time, in whale space.

o

Whale-shaped Eubeoa hugs the shore of mainland Greece. It fractured clear eons ago in some strike-slip quake that shook the big island free. At Halkida the channel narrows to the narrowest of cuts and Aristotle himself spent time there on and off through the years observing the tidal flow through the straight, first one way then the opposite, a river reversing itself, ass backward, plumbing the plumbing there. All that motion to no end, an ecstatic static.

o

But in the veins there are baffles of valves that eddy the spent blood flow upstream, fish ladders, toward the heart. The cells, those dimpled mauve lozenges, lining up like shallow draft coastal tankers en route, convoying oxygen away from the spongy anchorage of the lungs.

o

Around here somewhere the Greeks becalmed and beached, a thousand-island chain of triremes in irons, no way to be made on the way to Troy. It was that headland, or that headland there, where they kited Iphigenia into the sea, a debt owed to some god or other, to wake the breeze, to make it freshen. Troy would be thataway. Telling that story over and over, the tellers want what happened to happen differently, like running a length of film back and forth, see-sawing the eye, the eye hopping from one moment to the next, island frame to island frame, hoping that this time it will be all different, that other gods will intervene. As one did in Iphigenia's fall, intercepting her midair and turning her flesh insubstantial, her blood into aerosol, and transporting the mist of her beyond the Aegean to some

sacred steppes someplace where the history of history one steps
into is never, never the same twice.

o

Oh, let's blame the bloody sun, the bloody, bloody drink. Hell, it's
hell, this body in this in-between. The hot, you know, comes at you
in waves of layers, molten lava sandwiched between melting glass.
The blood, what there is of it, boils and pools, rises to the thinning
skin, the blush shedding sheets of heat, I shimmer in my own juices,
evaporate, another order of being, state of sacrifice. How did it go,
Winnie's witty turn of phrase, the eulogy's eulogy? Not the end. This
is not even the beginning of the end. The end of the beginning, then.
The end of the beginning.

o

I never see. I can't look. I won't watch. I'll turn away when they stop
up my arm, bend the elbow to tap this other drink. I am so wan, I
wane, not enough of any humor in me to fill a flute let alone a liter. I
am empty, empty enough. I am all out of going all out. I will clench
the rubber ball and focus on the horizon line out the porthole, and,
afterward, peel and eat the proffered orange orange. And if they ask
I already know my type. O, I will say, O. Negative. Donor. Universal.

—Michael Martone

Vanessa Gebbie

FIREWORKS AND BURNT TOAST
The Process of Opening Up Your Writing

Fireworks

You are outside in the dark, just a star or two. Somewhere, there are the sounds of a party on the other side of the street. The beat of a disco. Heightened talk, shouts, laughter. It is easy to turn away, leave that behind. Go back into the house.

Then—a firework. A single crack splits the air, a sizzle, a pause. A burst of stars, shimmering, falling in a fountain against the sky. The stars spiral and fall, painting the sky with trails of light.

Then it is over. You blink. But no—it is not over. Imprinted on your retina is a fountain of fire.

That is what a good flash ought to do. It should catch you as you turn away, hold you, and when you've finished reading, it should echo and resonate.

I have also likened flash fiction to diamonds and to non-safety matches. You just don't find diamonds the size of boulders. And a box of non-safety matches, when hit by accident, flares. That flare is what we want.

There is no secret about writing flash fiction. It is just a short story, but a short story that has been allowed by the writer to find its right shape

Vanessa Gebbie resides in East Sussex, UK. Her flash fiction and short fiction have been published widely and broadcast on BBC Radio, and she has received many writing awards (the Bridport Prize, *Fish International, Per Contra, Daily Telegraph,* Small Wonder Festival, Guildford Book Festival, to name a few). In 2008, she was final judge for the *Fish International One Page Competition.* A co-editor of *Cadenza* (a small press literary magazine) and a teacher of creative writing, Gebbie is also founder of *The Fiction Workhouse* online writers forum. Many of her prize-winning flash stories appear in her collection *Words from a Glass Bubble* (2008), which was long-listed for the Frank O'Connor Award. A second collection of flash fiction is forthcoming in fall 2009, also from Salt Publishing. Her site is www.vanessagebbie.com.

and length. Some stories need hundreds of thousands of words to be told. Think of *War and Peace, The Lord of the Rings*. And some need far fewer. Right at the other end of the spectrum we have Ernest Hemmingway's much-quoted six-word story:

"For sale: baby shoes, never worn."

I would argue that the effect of this last story on the reader may be as great if not greater than those epic books, wonderful as they are. It has the "moment"—the present situation—neatly wrapped up in a few words. In fact, wrapped up in the first four. A pair of baby shoes for sale. But that is the touch-paper, and the firework is about to blow. Add the last two words, and the rocket is launched, and in the reader's head are connections, pictures, discoveries, memories, sadnesses, understandings, anger, empathy, . . . *you* carry on. The list will be as long as there are readers, because the story was a door into a larger space.

Flash stories are far bigger than their minimal word counts might suggest. The worlds created so quickly are entire, deep. The characters are painted with a few deft brushstrokes, but are never stick-people. Go and read the selection of superb flashes listed at the back of this book, and you will see what I mean. But read slowly, as you might a poem. Let the words work their magic.

Kidnapping Your Reader

If you analyze it, a flash contains nothing different from other forms of fiction. The craft elements are the same, but are more concentrated. It is as though the elements have been put under a microscope, examined and reduced to only that which is utterly necessary.

I talked above about the firework catching the "reader" as she was about to turn away. And now I am going to focus on this element of flash. Because no matter how brilliant the rest of the show is, if you've lost your audience, you're playing to the air.

So how do competent flash writers kidnap their readers? They do so without the reader even being aware, through their opening sentences. And, before that even, through their titles.

The title is the planning stage of the kidnap. Look at the table of contents of any fiction collection on the Web or in print. Your eye will be drawn to certain titles and not others.

Which of these would you turn to first?

> *The Folk Singer Dreams of Time Machines*
> *The 13th Toast*
> *American Gothic*
> *My Dream*
> *Why This Isn't a Good Story to Tell*
> *The Bone Orchard*

I would go for *The Bone Orchard,* myself. I am drawn to the directness of it. But they all hold promise, intrigue, do they not? All except one. It is a safe bet that you did not pick *My Dream.* (The others are titles from Issue 21 of *SmokeLong Quarterly,* an excellent source of good flash fiction.)

Now, a few opening lines. The first two were picked at random from that same issue of *SmokeLong Quarterly,* then two are my own.

1. I was reading Flaubert when the angel spoke to me. ("The Angel's Visitation," by Corey Mesler)

2. Jackson's a chocolate lab. I brought him back from the no-kill this morning. ("Soap," by Katrina Denzer)

3. Kath said she had a brother she rescued from a bucket of water. ("Smoking Down There," *Eclectica,* Volume 10, No. 3)

4. Yesterday, I put on Simon's skin. ("Simon's Skin," *Fish International Prizewinner's Anthology 2006*)

All these openings introduce characters immediately. In those first lines, consider what you know already:

1. An intellectual, reading a French classical writer. Hears angels.

2. The narrator has rescued a dog from an animal shelter. A kindly act. The dog has escaped being put down.

3. Kath rescued her brother from what? Or at least she *says* she did, and the voice is slightly idiosyncratic.

4. The narrator did what? Put on someone else's skin?

But more than providing a beginning, each sentence intrigues you, the reader, and raises questions. What did that angel say to the narrator? Why? What has Flaubert got to do with it? What is special about Jackson? Why is the narrator telling us about him? How did Kath's brother nearly drown in a bucket? Does he actually do this in the story? How and why do you put on someone's skin? Who is telling this, and who is Simon?

With these questions in your head, you move on to the next sentences, and, like an insect slipping into a pitcher plant, the slide into the story has begun:

1. He was small like a worry stone.

2. I've always wanted a dog, but I did it more for Wylie.

3. But then Kath said lots of things.

4. I wanted to know what having a dick was like.

The first two examples are the openers to very short flashes of 161 and 162 words, respectively. Consummate examples of every word earning its place.

And, notice, no "weather forecasts"! How many stories do you read in which the first paragraph is a sort of weather forecast? *It was a sunny afternoon in April* or *It was snowing, and the wind was howling.* I would argue that unless it is seriously important, 99 percent of the time there is a much better way of opening any story. Especially in a flash. One of the reasons for this is that a "weather forecast" is not related to the story, except in very specific circumstances where the weather crosses over from background into character. Usually, a statement about the weather is a "toneless" one. Plain fact, delivered with no fictional color. The opening sentences of short stories have a vital role to play in setting the color or tone of the work, even more so in flash fiction.

And note that all the examples above start *in media res.* Using simple statements, those small sentences all introduce characters to whom something is happening. No clever writerly pyrotechnics, to go back to the fireworks image. Just straight storytelling.

And flashes are just that—storytelling. A strong, effective beginning starts a process that leads to a strong story.

Opening Up Your Writing

The telling of stories in small moments goes back to the dawn of time, does it not?

But flash writing is also a process. A fantastic, liberating writing process. One I use myself for many reasons, but more important, one I use constantly when I teach.

I have worked with many diverse groups of writers, from beginners to advanced. Flash writing techniques will always bring something positive and fresh to writers of all levels but is especially effective when working with those who have problems to overcome. For example, drug addicts in rehabilitation facilities and the homeless. I have worked with both groups extensively.

My work in this regard started in a series of residential rehabilitation centers for drug and alcohol addicts, run by an organization dedicated to helping long-term addicts to learn to live without drugs and to rehabilitate them into society. Creative writing is often used in rehab centers, and I was initially asked to run a trial series of sessions for a short while, a month.

These students had very limited attention spans due to the nature of their addictions and the physical symptoms associated with kicking their habits. I decided straightaway to use flash. Not only to incorporate the techniques into my facilitating, but also to encourage participants to work toward pieces of writing that were short, snappy, and "manageable." The sessions were so successful that the "month" lengthened to almost three years, and subsequently, I was invited to teach groups of homeless writers for a community publisher in my home city of Brighton and Hove, in the south of England.

From a standing start as very raw beginners, the groups went on to produce excellent writing that (with careful polishing) was of publishable quality. Publications indeed followed. The community publisher produced an anthology of writing from the homeless. More courses followed, with visits from established writers, courses whose objective was to encourage these writers to use their newfound skills to begin to earn a living. All of this was backed by local BBC radio and newspapers. And it all started with flash fiction.

It is interesting to look back and see how the initial sessions, the "make or break" sessions in rehab, were approached and organized.

Initially, I found the rehab students had very little self-esteem. They were absolutely positive they would never be able to do this thing called Creative Writing, and I heard such remarks as: *Writing is for clever people. Writing is for people who are OK.*

I told them very quickly that creative writing is no one's exclusive province. It is for everyone. I told them that I was not there to "judge" their work. This was not formal school (a time in their lives for which many had little fondness). I told them that spelling and grammar and handwriting were meaningless, that we were doing the *proper* stuff of making, creating. We could work on polishing and editing much later, together. They relaxed instantly, and within a few minutes we were all writing.

Flash as a process works for these disadvantaged groups because it is so inclusive. So instantaneous and, above all, fun.

Initially, everyone in the group was asked to produce words for prompts. At first, there would be an exchange like this:

> *Can't do it.*
> *Of course you can.*
> *How?*
> *Give me a word.*
> *What word?*
> *What did you have for breakfast?*
> *Burnt toast.*
> *There you are. Prompt One: **Burnt Toast.** Next?*

And everyone, laughing over finding words and finding it is easy, is then brave enough to write, with extraordinary results. Meaningful results that go far beyond the production of a few lines of writing. Their stories would often deal with their issues, things that bubbled up with little or no bidding as they wrote. Often, the words were raw and direct, sometimes painful. But always emotionally true and powerful.

Here is an example, the opening of a nonfiction flash by student Chris Ellis. This piece of work was polished and then subsequently accepted for publication by *Per Contra Journal of Literature and the Arts* and published in 2008:

History in His Hands

I still sleep with a knife under my pillow.

Do you know how it feels to sleep alone in a car park? A kind of freedom, but one that comes with a price? Choosing that spot between petrol, oil and piss? That moment when you suddenly snap out of sleep, last night's wine wearing off, and you sit there in the cold and the dark and you start to shake. You shake so much you can't even grasp that half-empty bottle.

It wasn't always like that. Once, I was the one who would cross the street at the sight of down and outs huddled in doorways.

Once, even, I touched history.

(The whole piece can be read at http://www.percontra.net/10ellis.htm.)

Again, there are no secrets. It is very easy to replicate the flash writing session with any writing group. You simply need one or two prompts, and they can be anything at all. A line of poetry you like for some reason. A newspaper photograph that your eye returned to again and again. A snippet of music. The closing lines of a song. A painting. A string of random words. And the trick is *not* to think about it for more than a second or two. Preferably not even that long. Just look at the prompt and write, letting the thoughts come freely and writing them down as they come.

On paper, this flash writing is easy. You just let your hand go, and don't self-censor. On screen, it can be a little more difficult, as some people (myself included) tend to edit as they write as it is so easy to do on a computer. But this ruins the creative flow, and there are some tricks to help you write freely on screen. Try turning off the screen and typing blind. (And do try not to hit the Caps Lock key.) On a laptop, turn the font color to white. At first you may feel rather uncomfortable but you will get used to it, and what spills out will be fresh, clear writing. Just "let go" and allow the mind to produce its own fabulous connections.

I have seen whole stories written in this way in a very few minutes.

And in my own case, I know that work produced like this has a liveliness that writing I agonize over for days just does not.

An Antidote for Writer's Block, and More Fireworks

Another bonus: once I had learned the technique of flash writing, I discovered that any period of writer's block has a new enemy. Times when I cannot write are very infrequent now, as all I have to do is turn off the screen and begin to write. Sooner or later the writing comes 'round to the piece I was finding hard to start, and avoiding.

It is so useful, too, for interrogating your characters, in times when you feel them slipping away from you. Again, turn off the screen and have a conversation with one of your characters. It is a certainty that after a while, your characters will begin to "talk" to you, and will reveal themselves in previously unforeseen ways.

Here in the UK, we have firework parties every November 5 for Guy Fawkes Night. We have bonfires in our gardens and on public spaces. At some point in the party, you may notice a crowd of children watching from a distance. A little shy, drawn to the warmth, the fun, but not knowing quite how to join in. Someone will walk over and hand out sparklers, hand-held fireworks that fizz and crackle with light.

It is a funny thing, but as soon as those sparklers are lit, what do the children do? Do they stand still, hold them out, and just watch them? A few, perhaps.

But the majority wheel their arms joyously and watch the shapes their sparklers make in the dark. They may write their names in sparks against the night sky, then shut their eyes to see the sparks on the inner screen of their eyelids.

Give yourself sparklers in the dark. Write stories that will flare and stay with the reader long after the show is finished.

❦

FLASH FICTION PROMPTS

Here are a few prompts for you to practice with, mostly taken from the poetry of Dylan Thomas. The first you will of course recognize. It is invariably a very successful writing prompt, and I have seen some beautiful work produced by many writers using this line as inspiration. The others are less well known, perhaps. And that is good. Even if words are unfamiliar (he invented his own vocabulary on occasion), see what your "writer's mind" does with these:

Do not go gentle into that good night

Unremembered skies and snows

Child of the short spark

Garden of time

Shawling out of the ground

Dancing with Cobweb

The story below is from work written instantaneously to the prompt *Dancing with Cobweb* by a writer new to flash techniques, Douglas Bruton. He was wary, but willing to try. This story was completed in less than 20 minutes, consists of just 635 words, and is unedited apart from typos.

Study his wonderful flowing images and the very real, achy story that developed from the prompt. (By the way, a "chanter" is part of a set of bagpipes. Bruton is a Scot.)

A STORY EXAMPLE

Dancing with Cobweb

I am there in the barn, small moonlight breaking through a high window, the thick air warm, and the horses snorting derision. There is music playing, my papa's fingers fluttering like frightened birds over the holes of his chanter and my mother singing at the sink, or at the oven. I can see in my head her hair pinned back, but a miscreant lock of grey falling limp across her face, and her cheeks flushed and her eyes full of out-of-reach dreams. And she is singing, and my papa hunched forwards in his chair, one foot tapping on the wooden floor, and blowing familiar music into the night.

And I am dancing, there in the barn, always dancing when there is music, my feet following the rhythm of my papa's drumming foot, and me dancing in and out of the blue light of the moon, like it is a dream. And it is a dream, for I am holding someone in my arms and she moves with me, her feet in step with mine, shuffling through the spilled straw, and my hand at her waist, or where I imagine a girl's waist to be. And I wonder if there is someone other than my heavy-footed father dancing in my mother's head, if that is the dream I see moving behind her eyes when she sings.

And there is a girl in my arms. I can feel one small hand clasped palm to palm in mine, can smell her hair if I lean in close, and the music turns us from one end of the barn to the other. And my faint heart runs breathless ahead of me, so that my head spins and the dirt-floor tilts and I fall. And she falls with me, and I hear laughter, my mother laughing, and the music broken, and the horses stamping their impatience.

And the girl's hand down the front of my trousers then, with my hand, and there on a bed of straw in my father's barn she gifts me make-believe kisses. And I see spiders in her mussed up hair, her breath smelling sweet, like new cut straw, and my own breath snatched.

And when I close my eyes I can see her, a girl I follow to school most days, my steps in hers only at a distance. Every day for almost a year now, the distance never shortened. She moves away from me, and that is a kind of dance, too, though there is no music playing. And I hurry after. But though I see her plain as though she was really there in the barn and it was day, though I see her in my head, every dress she ever wore, the movement of her hair as she walks, the way she holds her books pressed to her chest as though she has dreams, too, hidden, there where her heart is—though I see all of this clear as though she is there, I do not know her name.

What you always dreaming for, my papa says when he catches me. There's work needs doing, and you always dreaming. Like you was a girl. You want to clear those cobwebs out of your head and see sense, boy. No dream is gonna get you a woman to cook for you, and to wash for you and to keep your bed warm.

And my mother's eyes, still blue, filled with unspilled tears when she hears him say this. And the girl in my head, I call her Cobweb just for fun, and there in the barn, with the horses quiet again, and my father paused for breath and no music playing, I call her name and feel my body arch and the dream is warm and wet in my hand.

—Douglas Bruton

Jennifer Pieroni

SMART SURPRISE IN FLASH FICTION

As an editor of flash fiction—highly condensed, yet fully realized narratives—I seek stories with smart surprises. There are many types of surprise that are not smart, such as those that deliberately mislead the reader, or those that spend three-fourths of the word count positioning the story for a punch line or twist ending.

Instead of focusing on those elements, a writer's primary focus should be on the narrative line (or the arc) of the piece. Regardless of whether a particular piece of flash fiction is encapsulating a moment or spanning many years, it simply must be brief. Once a strong storyline is intact, the writer should go about peppering the piece with smart surprises for her reader. Smart surprise isn't at the beginning, the middle, or at the ending. Surprise can be, and must be, everywhere. If it is, your work will not only get noticed, it will also be remembered.

Two effective vehicles for smart surprise are *language* and *image.*

Language

Excellent flash fiction displays a true mastery of language. Not only must the writer be precise, but she must also engage the reader in a response to

Jennifer Pieroni was born in Framingham, Massachusetts, and currently resides a bit further north in Salem with her husband, Adam. Pieroni graduated from Emerson College's Writing, Literature, and Publishing program, where she studied flash fiction with Pamela Painter (p. 1). These early experiences with the form inspired her and her husband to establish in 2001 *Quick Fiction,* a literary journal (ranked #4 in New England by the *Boston Globe,* 2008) featuring stories and narrative prose poems under 500 words. As editor in chief, Pieroni manages the editorial process and guides the aesthetic of the journal. In 2008, she co-founded The Parlor: North Shore's Independent Writing Studio (also based in Salem), and works to ensure that its programs are high quality and sustainable. Pieroni's flash fiction has been published both in print and online.

the work. As in a sonnet, every word in every line matters in the mathematical sense. Further, as with poetry more generally, I see excellent writers as having a certain flair for words, a real intent to use them to provoke and, dare I say, surprise the reader. Examples of using language to create smart surprise could include: odd words; uncommon word pairings or de-packaging common phrases; invented words; and conscious crafting of the rhythm of words when brought together into a sentence.

Image

Just one strong, central image can make the difference between a story being forgettable and being one that stays with the reader forever. Therefore, a writer should carefully select the images she brings to the forefront of the story's visual palette. Memorable images are natural elements of a scene that are developed to shock readers out of a routine feeling, mood, or expectation. When this shock, or jolt, has been achieved, images can actually carry an incredible amount of emotional weight within a story and extend that heavy emotion to the reader.

To illustrate smart surprise by a very smart writer, I've included Szilvia Molnar's story "Mine" as a story example. Notice how the common phrase "*My oh my*" is used in an unexpected way. Further, the phrase "scent of giggles" and use of "note" as a synonym for the bite mark are both startlingly distinctive. Finally, Molnar's incredible images— "braided her hair with yours" and "bruise that had the backside of a rainbow"—both astonish the reader while expanding the emotional value of the story.

Ultimately, I couldn't agree more with what Sam Ruddick said in his essay "Tiny Revelation" (published online by *971 Menu*, 2007). He writes, "We seek to be surprised, not by a trick ending, but by the feeling we get from reading the piece. At their best, these stories will make you pause, tilt your head and say 'oh,' providing a tiny revelation, a new way of seeing, or a new way of saying something you've seen and been unable to articulate."

By searching for and selecting language and images so fresh they surprise the reader, writer's engage in a process that will inevitably produce stronger flash fiction. And the resulting work will be so uniquely their own that writers just might surprise themselves.

⌒*⌒*

A FLASH FICTION EXERCISE

The objective of this exercise is to make your story noticeable and memorable by using smart surprise as an element throughout the piece. The two vehicles you will use are language and image. The greatest villain of smart surprise is the word package or the clichéd image. These are common phrases, such as "all of a sudden," or familiar images, such as "a tear streamed over her cheek." After examining Molnar's story, use your creativity, your ear for language, and a really good thesaurus to look over a piece of your own flash fiction (or longer fiction) that has been rejected or that has received a lukewarm response. Revise any clichéd phrases and images, with the goal now of surprising the reader with their freshness. If it's a longer story, try to cut it down to about 500 words.

A STORY EXAMPLE

Mine

I used to call her *My oh my* because she was the girl that braided her hair with yours and she was the one that woke up in the morning with grass stains on her ankles and dew on her shoulders.

In high school she came up to me and grabbed me by the arm. We walked up stairs that lead to the fourth floor, and sat on a bench next to the darkroom. I looked at the long row of lockers and how its locks seemed so pleased being together. She pulled up my sleeve and bit me 'til it left a mark. She left me a scent of giggles and a note on my skin saying: "Now you'll remember me."

I walked around for five days with a bruise that had the backside of a rainbow and screams of *My oh my*. I've never been so angry before.

—Szilvia Molnar, from *Quick Fiction*

Randall Brown

MAKING FLASH COUNT

Somewhere, I lost count. Ten thousand. Twelve thousand. Fifteen thousand. Call it "a lot." Almost all of it unpublished. That's one of the joys of working with flash fiction as a teacher, editor, writer, submissions reader, and workshop participant. You get to read a lot of flash fiction, all of it seemingly without any clear definition except one: a word count. One hundred exactly. Not a word more than 750. At some point (500 or less?) it's microfiction, a few words more it's sudden fiction, then flash. Or maybe it's flash, then sudden? At a 1,000+ word count, it's most likely, but not always, going to the short story editor. Go figure.

When I think of my favorite flash writers, I like to imagine they are aware of how each word of that count lessens the possibility of another one. I like to think that they begin with the idea of brevity, a very tiny space, think of how largely they might fill it. I like to think they wonder how to make something so little count so much. Can a tiny thing matter as much as a big one? Imagine a flash mattering as much as a novel, 300 words that add up to 30,000.

There's always that mystery of the flashes that work, the ones that matter in some seemingly inexplicable way. But, as a teacher of flash fic-

Randall Brown is author of the award-winning flash fiction collection *Mad to Live* (Flume Press, 2008). He teaches at Saint Joseph's University and holds an MFA from Vermont College, and has received Pushcart, O. Henry, and Best of the Web nominations. His work has appeared or is forthcoming in numerous journals, including *Cream City Review, Quick Fiction, Hunger Mountain, Connecticut Review, Saint Ann's Review, Evansville Review, Laurel Review, Dalhousie Review, Clackamas Literary Review,* and *Vestal Review*. An editor with *SmokeLong Quarterly* (an online journal devoted exclusively to flash fiction), his articles on flash appear online. Born in Camp Hill, Pennsylvania, Brown and his family now live outside of Philadelphia, where he was a featured presenter on flash fiction at the 2008 Philadelphia Writers Conference.

tion, I'm constantly looking for the explicable, that something to tell my students who don't ask, "What is flash?" but instead, "How do I make it flash?"

Charles Baxter, in his book *Burning Down the House*, writes about a character's confrontation with his or her Other, calling such meetings an encounter between "two characters who hardly belong together…forced to inhabit the same frame" (114). That sense of an encounter, of hardly belonging together, and the sharing of a tiny space inform a number of my favorite flashes along with many of my own, especially early on in my flash-writing career: A husband encounters his pregnant wife eating ants. A man encounters, in his date's freezer, thumb-size, foil-wrapped packages with taped-on men's names. A brother and sister encounter a drought-drained river with rocks like a pathway from bank-to-bank. A woman looks out her window and encounters a workman crapping on her lawn. Two kids in a willow tree encounter a bow-hunter.

At *SmokeLong Quarterly*, where I've worked since 2004 with founder Dave Clapper and his terrific cast of staff and guest editors, so many of my favorite flashes begin with these types of encounters—highly charged, interesting, rare. In "Outer Space," by Tom Saunders, children encounter their mother during a meteor shower. Ellen Parker's "Metallic" begins, "I told this new man I would have sex with him only through the fence." The reader confronts "five fat men in a hot tub" at the beginning of Jeff Landon's "Hot Tub" flash. Steven Gullion's narrator in "BiC" encounters, in his cat's litter box, "a ballpoint pen rising, at a jaunty angle, from the sand."

What I especially love about flash is that constant reminder of time and words running out, how flash does not permit the drawn-out encounter, scene after scene in which the character acts and fails, acts and fails, acts and fails, acts and fails before finally recovering something like knowledge. Here is the demand of the flash form: to find in compression what cannot be found otherwise, to view the constriction of time and space as a need for urgency and profundity.

So, the flash writer thinks of an encounter, the seldom seen one, say, that ballpoint pen in a litter box. In the flash encounter, tension builds and develops in the intensity of the shared, confined space. It's one thing to say to a character: "You get 5,000 words to figure this out. You get three failed attempts before the light goes off." It's quite another thing for the flash writer, who might say to his character, "You get 500 words. That's it. There's a BiC pen in your cat's litter box. Figure it out. Make something of it. Make it matter."

Of course, no one way to write a flash exists; but this has been one way I've discovered flash. First, there's that encounter, something original and remarkable. To give that encounter the sense of mattering, characters often encounter the very things that will lead them to profundity, vision, and newness. Rather than waiting for the end only, the writer can twist expectations throughout. Each new word, each new sentence can struggle to bring the character and reader deeper both into the encounter and into its meaning to the character(s). Throughout, the constraints of word and time and space drive the flash toward its final sense. At the end, something gets figured out, by the writer, the story's character(s), its readers.

One of my very first flashes involved the idea of a husband discovering his pregnant wife eating ants. I use this flash as an example because I remember so clearly the questions I asked of myself as the flash began and moved toward its conclusion. As I was just learning flash, I first began thinking of what to hide from the reader. Her pregnancy? Their previous miscarriages? That the baby was already miscarried? And so on.

With the help of writers wiser than I, I decided that whatever I wanted to hide should be the very things I confront, right from the outset. So this story begins:

> I find Maggie squatting on the kitchen floor beside the door to the garage. My eyes always go to her belly first, as if she has swallowed a globe. There've been two miscarriages, both early. Never have we gotten so far. Then I notice she's picking something off the floor, putting it in her mouth. Get closer. They surround her. Hundreds of them. Ants. Maggie is eating ants.

So, next came the decision of how the husband should react. At first, I had him furious, screaming, slamming the door, leaving her. And then I thought, what if I went against expectation? What if, instead, he reacts like this: "Really? They sell crickets at pet stores. I could get some."

Here, I thought of all those millions of stories that have preceded mine, all the expectations of readers and editors. How could I surprise them with this story without resorting to gimmicks and tricks? I felt that the husband's reaction allowed the flash to go deeper into the nature of their love, the poignancy of their losses, the strength of their bond and their endless hope. It found within the characters something surprising and touching (hopefully). It looked within rather than without for its punch lines.

That led me to the question of "So what?" So what—that this guy confronts a bug-eating pregnant wife? Why, of all the encounters in the world, did he get this one? Here, for me, comes the joy of writing flash, of setting up a situation without knowing how the characters will act, not knowing what will happen when they do. It surprised me that he went out and bought those crickets, and as he paused in the garage, staring at them, I gazed at them too, pondering them, their meaning for him, the whys we often ask of the gods.

Why am I here? Why am I staring at a bag full of crickets, while my wife waits upstairs, a baby struggling for life within her?

What did it all mean?—her hunger for bugs, his attempt to make everything okay for her and the baby, the baby still holding on to life? What could one do when faced with such a Fate? His questions merged with my own, each word, it would seem, bringing both of us closer to figuring something out, a fleeting thing maybe, but something.

I picture the bugs slithering down her throat, at the bottom, a baby open-mouthed—a miracle baby. Dozens of times, the brown bleeding began, and we were told she was lost, only to see her on the ultrasound, hear the beat beat of her heart. How useless and helpless I feel during these races to the hospital, as if there's nothing I can do for them.

He brings the crickets upstairs. She's bleeding. Heavier. I remember feeling the limit of the word count, of time and space narrowing and ticking and all the other things time and space do. I remember how much I loved flash in that moment, with the end encroaching upon me from the very outset. It needed to end. But how?

Should it end with his eating a cricket?

Should it end with uncertainty and hope, such as with this line: "We agree that has to be a good sign."

Should it end with certainty of the baby living—or not?

So, I went back, thought about (1) the question the I, as writer, had been trying to work out with this story; and (2) the question the I, as character, had been working to resolve.

What was the central issue for this character? I found it here: "How useless and helpless I feel during these races to the hospital, as if there's nothing I can do for them." What could he possibly do for them? And why did these characters suffer for me? For what reason did I push them through these actions and conflicts? What did I want to know?

Maybe I wanted to know what he wanted to know, "What can he do for them?"

Terrified that the answer might truly be "nothing."

But there was something, wasn't there?

There was this:

A blur—the car ride, Maggie holding the bag of crickets, tapping against the plastic, then opening it, taking one out. "She's still hungry."

The breakneck drive, the crickets, the hospital waiting for our arrival—it's all part of the blur, something to hide the truth from both of us, that nothing matters except the desires of Fate for our baby to live. But that's nothing to tell Maggie.

"It has to be a good sign," I tell her.

"It does, doesn't it?" Maggie answers, then opens her mouth and feeds our baby's desire.

In Baxter's analyses of encounters and the Other, he finds that the characters often discover, at the end, an emergent "precious thing" (113). The first story I remember reading is the Sesame Street one in which Grover keeps trying to prevent page after page from being turned because he's afraid of the monster at the end of the book. He uses stronger and stronger material to bind the book, to prevent the horrible end in which he must face the monster. We turn that final page and Grover discovers himself.

For my students and my characters, I imagine that to be one of the emergent, precious things to be found at the end of that count after count of words—the recognition that the something waiting for us there lies not without, but within, that we have confronted and encountered that something in a unique, profound way, and that those monstrous things, when brought to light, are actually ours, have always been so, since the very beginning.

A FLASH FICTION EXERCISE

Study Myfanwy Collins's flash story below, paying particular attention to all that Jessie, reader, and writer confront and ultimately discover on this Christmas Eve: the infection, the hallucinations, the subway fellow, the absorption, the Bert without its Ernie. Note the relationship among them, how each one brings Jessie, reader, and writer closer to revelation and understanding. Then, in the first paragraph of your own flash story, have a character encounter something original and remarkable. Make what's encountered be the very confrontation that will lead the character and/or reader to that emergent precious thing. Twist expectations throughout. Try to have each new word, each new sentence bring the character and reader deeper into the encounter and its meaning to the character(s). Be aware of the constraints of word and time and space as the flash struggles toward sense. End it when something gets figured out, by you, your character(s), its readers. And, finally, be sure to give the flash the appropriately interesting, evocative title, something like Daphne Buter's "He Wrote Sixteen Pencils Empty."

A STORY EXAMPLE

I Am Holding Your Hand

It was Christmas Eve and Jessie was hallucinating. She was ten and her tonsils were infected, but she would not be one of the lucky ones who had the operation to remove the dangling bits and then live on ice cream afterwards. No, she would suffer through with the help of antibiotics. Her tonsils would not have a chance to grow back.

Jessie's mother had her tonsils removed as a girl, but they grew back, a fact Jessie found both disturbing and titillating. That humans might have body parts which grew back. Could this mean there was a cure for death?

When she was much older Jessie would be on a subway with a fellow from Germany. He would tell her how his body had become covered in lumps when he was nineteen. Upon investigation the doctors found that the lumps contained hair and bone and teeth. He had absorbed his own twin while he was in the womb.

But Jessie had no twin, absorbed or otherwise.

Her throat ached, her fever spiked. It was the first year her father was not there on Christmas Eve channeling Louis Armstrong on their way back from midnight mass. Instead, he was in his apartment across town. Earlier in the day he'd had the girls over and brought them one after the other into the bathroom and showed them the presents he had gotten for each. Jessie's big sister would receive a stuffed kangaroo, which Jessie coveted. It was small, its fur velveteen. She thought it would work nicely with her Barbies. They might travel to Australia. Skipper might meet a priest in the Outback. Fall in love.

Jessie would spend Christmas day on the couch, sweating, seeing things that were not there, listening to her mother play the new Neil Diamond record over and over until it seemed Neil Diamond had been absorbed into their living room and family.

When her father came, he would bring her a present. A Bert, but no Ernie. Bert was not too much smaller than she was, his head pointy, his clothes removable, but best not removed as underneath he was featureless—a stuffed pillow.

How old was Bert? Wasn't he a grown man? What an odd choice. His expression was curmudgeonly, unlovable. She feigned appreciation, though her only feeling toward Bert was pity. He was like her father now, living a life without the company of women.

Her father would die in May, in the night and alone, with not

even Ernie by his side to hold his hand, to tell him to hold on. No
Ernie to remind him of those times when he was loved.

Remember when you were a boy? You had a white pony and a
wide-brimmed hat. Think about that pony, that hat. Focus. I am
holding your hand.

—Myfanwy Collins, from *Monkeybicycle*

Lex Williford

FORTY STORIES IN THE DESERT

*Flash fiction is a story-poem with three sharp turns in a labyrinth leading
to a precipice and a mirror and a reflection, half beast and half human,
and the only weapon, the only way out: a magic ball of twine.*

—Lex Williford, *Hayden's Ferry Review,* Special Section: Flash Fiction (2003)

Twenty years ago, I wrote a 15-page story titled "Pendergast's Daughter."
Hard as I struggled with many drafts over the long, hot Alabama summer
of 1988, the story just wasn't very good. I've tried for many years in my
work to understand the roots of family violence, but I couldn't make cred-
ible the random violence of the narrator's potential father-in-law-to-be.
Frustrated and defeated, feeling I'd wasted months on a dead-end story,
I put it away, essentially abandoning it. I would never look at that draft
of the story again.

But toward the end of that summer, in a flash, a single thought occurred
to me while I was mowing the backyard: *You can do it all in one page.*

In the kind of dream state physical labor has always put me in—my
freckled forearms speckled with wet flecks of itchy grass, sweat stinging
my eyes—I rushed inside to my study, grabbed a yellow legal pad, and
rewrote the entire story in a single sitting of 15 minutes.

Lex Williford spent the first six months of his life in El Paso, Texas, and didn't return to
live there again until the age of 50. He holds an MFA from the University of Arkansas and
has taught writing for many years. *Macauley's Thumb* (1994) was co-winner of the Iowa
School of Letters Award for Short Fiction. Described by one reviewer as a "master of
characterization," Williford has stories anthologized in W. W. Norton's *Flash Fiction* (1992);
The Iowa Award: The Best Stories, 1991–2000 (2001); *The Eloquent Short Story* (2004); and
elsewhere. He is co-editor, with Michael Martone (p. 45), of the popular *Scribner Anthology
of Contemporary Short Fiction* (2007) and the accompanying *Touchstone Anthology of
Contemporary Creative Nonfiction* (2007). Williford is director of the University of Texas–El
Paso's online MFA program.

When I finished, I heard the mower still roaring in the yard and went back outside into the steamy heat to finish the last few rows of grass.

Returning to my air-conditioned study 30 minutes later, excited but afraid to look at what I'd written, I reread the story—smudged with red clay, sweat, and dead grass—and realized it was finished, a final draft, or something close to it, a gift delivered to me in one page, almost exactly as if I'd written it in a fever, except for a few words I'd changed here and there. Later, the story was published in *Quarterly West*, then went on to be reprinted in many anthologies and to be translated into several languages, including Farsi.

All these years later, I'm still convinced that I would never have written the short short story without having written the longer story and failing. Worrying the story, pushing that Sisyphean boulder up a hill only to watch it roll back down again and again, was all in preparation for this flash of insight: to focus on a single moment, a moment that changed everything for me—a flash fiction written before the term became popular, the first of many I've written since.

For me, flash fiction usually begins in image and ends with something akin to the lyricism of poetry. But what sets it apart, say, from a prose poem, is that the story must turn *dramatically*, must have a complete reversal of some sort, a surprise so stunning and rich that it could only happen in a story, and that reversal is usually carried by powerful, unforgettable images. Like a wood splinter under a thumbnail, such images are barbed and remain inextricable no matter how long one might probe beneath bleeding flesh to dig them out.

A few years back, I received a fellowship to the Helene Wurlitzer Foundation: forty days and nights in a nice casita in Taos, New Mexico, where I'd have the solitude and time to write in the cool, sage-scented foothills of the Sangre de Christo Mountains. It all sounded a little too biblical for me—40 days in the desert—so I decided to write one story for every day I would be there. Forty stories in 40 days.

Every morning I got up and sat on the front porch of my casita drinking coffee and trying to think of images to begin with as I listened to magpies squawking from the pines, and then I set my watch's timer and tried to write an entire story within 15 minutes. (The magpies looked a bit like nuns so I wrote two nun stories, one about a good nun and one about a very bad nun.) I spent the rest of the day playing around with what I'd written in that flash of insight, expanding, then contracting, each story, crafting each one on my computer, sometimes making significant changes, until I had something satisfactory, or better. I ended up taking a few days off here and there to hike up Lobos Peak in the Taos Ski Valley or to drive to Angel Fire or Eagle's Nest or Red River or to take mud baths and sit bubbling in the mineral waters at Ojo Caliente, but I wrote 36 stories in those 40 days.

For years, I've asked my students to do something similar: to write what I call 15-minute fictions, at least one a week for the first five weeks of class.[1] And my students have produced some remarkably powerful stories from these exercises, beginning with short shorts as heuristic devices that encourage the discovery of images, characters, and storylines. The beauty of these exercises, these little thought experiments, is that students can fail and succeed more often, and abandoning stories that don't burn like glowing briquettes in their bellies seems less of a loss.

More important, writing these short shorts in such an intense flash helps make the story focus on the most important moments in the story, moments one can build upon.

Ultimately, with much revision, these 15-minute exercises can become published short shorts, or they can accumulate heft and depth, evolving into longer short stories, or—because they focus on the most intense dramatic reversals in fiction—they can become the building blocks of even longer prose forms such as the novella and novel. Will the novel-in-short-short-stories, like the novel-in-stories that began in the mid-eighties, evolve into a distinctive and exciting new form? It wouldn't surprise me at all if that evolution has already begun.

---

[1] One could also call these *sketches*—like those my architect father used to rough out on layers of tracing paper to conceptualize ideas that he would eventually turn into pages of working drawings on blueprint.

A FLASH FICTION PROMPT

Ror·schach test (rôr'shäk', -shäкн.) *n.*
A psychological test in which a subject's interpretations of a series of standard inkblots are analyzed as an indication of personality traits, preoccupations, and conflicts.
—*American Heritage Dictionary,* 4th ed. (Houghton Mifflin, 2002)

Based upon the well-known (and occasionally maligned)[2] Rorschach inkblot test, originally designed by Swiss psychiatrist Hermann Rorschach (1884–1922), this exercise is essentially an image factory whose raw material comes directly from the dark diamond mines of the unconscious. The main difference here is that, rather than using the hard-to-find original inkblots created by Rorschach, systematized by psychologist John E. Exner in a scoring system used by many psychiatrists over the last 30 years, I ask my students to generate their own inkblots, and that's just part of the fun.

Supplies:

1. A bottle of ink. (You can buy ink at any arts and crafts store, colored or otherwise, but I've had the best luck with black India ink. The only problem is that it's permanent and hard to get off your hands and clothes, so be careful.)

2. Typing paper. (Actually, I prefer white card stock, because the ink bleeds through anything less heavy, but any kind of paper will do.)

3. A cardboard box top or newspaper to keep your inkblot from staining your table.

4. Lots of paper towels and rubbing alcohol, just in case you get ink on your hands.

---

[2] I say *maligned* here not because the images don't come from unconscious sources but because some skeptics believe that several psychiatric vehicles for *interpreting* these tests—ten original, highly ambiguous inkblots created in 1921—are questionable. Because the test has been administered to so many over so many years, however, its findings are well-supported in science, a useful if not altogether accurate means of diagnosing mental illnesses of all kinds, but as my example story suggests, I'm a bit of a skeptic, too, mainly because the tests pathologize imagination in ways that are potentially dangerous.

Procedure:

1. Get two pieces of white paper, one to make your inkblot on, the other to write on.

2. On one sheet of paper, number one through ten.

3. Lay the other sheet of paper on a tabletop covered in newspaper or cardboard.

4. Squeezing out a few drops of India ink, let them randomly plop onto the paper.

5. Fold the paper in half, make a strong crease and smooth the paper flat, and then unfold it.

6. Stare at the inkblot you've made, turning it any direction you wish. Write down every image you see. Focus on the images themselves, *not* on how they make you feel. In other words, don't write down abstractions or try to interpret the feelings the images provoke: *angry, sad, goofy*. Instead, write down as specifically and vividly as possible *only* what you see. Try to avoid writing down clichés or pop-culture references: aliens, vampires, Spider Man, Donald Trump. But don't censor yourself. If the images are strange, frightening, disturbing, even ludicrous, no problem. You're doing just exactly what you're supposed to do. And as the late, great Ray Bradbury used to say: "Don't think." Just write what you see and let the images convey *on their own* what you're feeling.[3]

7. When you've written down at least ten images, let the list sit awhile and try not to think about it too much.

---

[3] Theoretically, Rorschachs are projections of the writer's unconscious emotions. When we dream, our emotions are often projected as images or metaphorical situations: we're naked in a public place, for example, showing that we feel exposed, vulnerable, if not literally, as least metaphorically. T. S. Eliot writes, "The only way of expressing emotion in the form of art is by finding an 'objective correlative'; in other words, a set of objects, a situation, a chain of events which shall be the formula of that particular emotion; such that when the external facts, which must terminate in sensory experience, are given, the emotion is immediately evoked" ("Hamlet and His Problems," reprinted at www.bartleby.com/200/sw9.html). In other words, the image itself *carries* the emotion and *does all the work on its own*. To interpret for the reader is to mistrust the reader.

8. Then sit down, set a timer or your watch, and write a 15-minute fiction using as many of the images as you can. If you can't put the images into the stories directly, use them as surprising metaphors and similes.

Example Inkblot:[4]

Because I wanted to push myself a bit for *The Rose Metal Press Field Guide*, I tried to create more than ten items, and because I already knew the story I was going to write would be about an actual Rorschach test with a fictional patient in a fictional psychiatrist's office, I set myself a single ground rule: I couldn't use the images for anything but the story itself, not for the Rorschach in the story, or I'd be cheating.

Here's the inkblot I used:

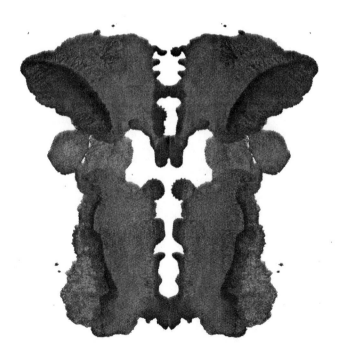

---

[4] Before you create your own inkblot, you might want to write everything down you see in the same inkblot I used, then compare it to my list. Did you see the same images I saw? Others?

When I got stuck or stopped seeing images, I turned the page around in all four directions, like this:

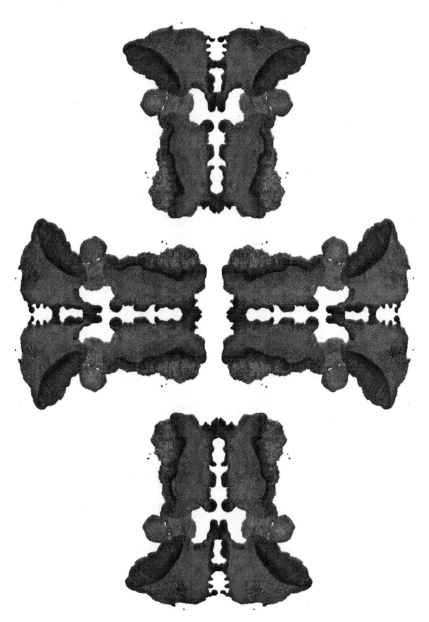

When I'd finished my list—about 15 images—I wanted to challenge myself further, so I asked my wife and in-laws to come up with their own lists, and I combined them all into a list of over 30 surprising images, all of which I decided to include in my story:

1. Mantis face
2. Skull shadow
3. Octopus
4. Saxophone
5. Giraffe
6. Death's-head hawk moth
7. Gazelle
8. Grim Reaper
9. A cracked-shell turtle mashed on a two-lane highway
10. Mountain range reflected in a lake
11. Luna moth
12. Caterpillar
13. Stew pot
14. Theater mask
15. A skull and crossbones
16. Thistle
17. Violin
18. Claw-foot bathtub
19. Hooded monk
20. A face half-submerged in water
21. Bedpost finial
22. Pitcher plant
23. Venus flytrap
24. Bee hive
25. Paper wasp nest
26. Papoose
27. Executioner's mask
28. Platypus
29. Shetland pony with a long mane
30. Squinting bald man
31. Lions on a coat of arms

The writing assignment I'd given myself seemed a bit daunting at first, but once I got the first image—"mantis-faced psychiatrist"— the rest came fairly quickly as I began crossing out the images I'd already written.

A STORY EXAMPLE

Rorschach

My sister Maddie's new mantis-faced psychiatrist had asked her
to take the test a month ago, she told me across a crumby table,
her hands trembling as she chewed on a poppy-seed bagel at our
favorite place to go whenever I visited her in the city, Zabar's on 80th
and Broadway, a smear of lox and cream cheese on her lower lip like
she'd bitten a caterpillar in half.

"I'm not so good with tests," she told Dr. Gazelle. "Worried for
years my ex was HIV positive. Never liked needles, not since my kid
brother died of leukemia. Prefer denial and booze. Like my father
that way, I guess. Got test anxiety with the state psychological exam
and failed it like all the acting tests I took in college."

She smiled at me like a theater mask as she told the story. She'd
made a living for years faking being happy in musicals, singing with
her liquid-silver voice about mountains reflected in clear lakes.

None of Maddie's psychiatrists before Dr. Gazelle could agree on
a diagnosis: bipolar disorder, a mixed depression-anxiety disorder,
obsessive compulsive personality disorder, even the same rare form
of epilepsy Dostoevsky had, but they'd all been wrong, at least about
the meds. Lithium, Prozac, Depacote, anticonvulsives, you name
it; none of them worked, mix or match, except to make her fly into
hypomania or sleep all day, except to give her the cottonmouth or
make her hands shake like luna moths.

The famous Dr. Gazelle on Park Avenue had taken her on pro
bono, she told me, because she was desperate—"a fascinating, stub-
born case," he said—and he'd seen a few of her shows. But by then
she was starting to feel like his goddamn lab rat.

The test was simple enough, she told me. All she had to do was
look at ten inkblots reproduced on cardboard and tell Gazelle what
she saw.

"Don't see a damn thing," she said at first, not even the common
things ordinary people saw: butterflies or bats, faces and vases, depending on whether they focused on the black or the white like that
optical illusion thingy in her old psych texts.

She glanced up at a potted plant on Gazelle's desk. A Venus fly-trap? A pitcher plant? And the vase itself looked like a stew pot. On the wall were all of Gazelle's diplomas—Yale, NYU, Johns Hopkins—and something in a fancy gilded frame like a bedpost finial. A skull and crossbones? A framed coat of arms with lions on a shield? A Shetland pony with a long mane? She squinted, but she couldn't tell. Then she realized it was the good doctor's wife, frowning a little, long-necked and anorexic as a giraffe. And the wallpaper behind the frame had a repeated pattern in yellow like that story she'd read in Freshman Comp about the crazy woman in the attic: A papoose or a platypus? A paper wasp nest or a beehive? Death's-head hawk moths and thistles?

And that's what got her started. It didn't matter what she saw, she said. The only thing that mattered was acing the test, showing this uppity uptown shrink how smart she was, how goddamn observant.

At first all she saw on the card the doctor held up was her own face half-submerged in water, like that time she'd settled back into her claw-foot tub in Long Island City, trying to see how far under she could go without drowning, water trickling into her nostrils until she came up, coughing. Chickenshit as always to go all the way. She sure as hell wasn't going to tell him about that.

She told Gazelle the first thing that came to mind—no, she couldn't remember what it was *now*, she told me—and then the doctor said what doctors always say: "And how does that make you feel?"

"Pissed," she said, and went on.

She could feel herself heating up and the images in the cards coming at her like cars whooshing over a turtle mashed on a two-lane highway, crushing her. She saw a thousand things and named them all, the words blotting out her life, everything she knew and ever would know. And she couldn't stop, not for the whole hour, not until Gazelle told her that her time was up.

"Did I pass?" Maddie asked him, and smiled. "Schizophrenic psychotic neurotic, right?"

She never returned to his office again.

A skull-shadowed homeless guy, looking like a hooded monk and wrinkled and bald as an octopus, pressed his greasy nose against the window glass right outside our table at Zabar's, shielding his eyes as he looked inside.

Maddie had long since stopped talking to me, staring down at her own trembling hands, when she saw him squinting at her. She waved at him, smiled. He had something tucked under his hole-pocked hoodie. A violin? A saxophone? I couldn't tell.

"Travis," she said, "meet the Grim Reaper, the Grand Executioner. He's been following me everywhere since."

The homeless guy was ranting, but when he saw Maddie smile, he smiled back, black-toothed, and waved at her.

"Poor old guy's hungry," she said, and wiped the smear of cream cheese from her mouth.

Then she stood from our table and went back to the long line at the counter to buy him an Everything bagel on our way out.

—Lex Williford

Robert Shapard

STAYING TRUE TO THE IMAGE

My best flashes come from focusing on the image that prompted the story in the first place. For example, recently I based a story on a dream fragment, a baby born with tattoos. For some reason this odd image resonated with me, so I started building a story around it, thinking of how such a thing could happen and who would care and what might be at stake. I wrote it with realistic detail, and it worked well enough to win a Best of the Net award.

This way of writing flashes may seem easy, at least in principle, but it isn't always. As with any writing, there are questions. Some of the ones I get asked are: How is this approach any different from writing a poem? Or a longer story? Or even a novel? And what exactly do you mean by "staying focused on an image"?

On the poetry side, writer A. Van Jordan has said of his creative approach, "The image is what comes to mind first. Trying to correlate that image with an emotion is the rest of the process" (*Texas Monthly*, June 2008, p. 30). This reminds me that Grace Paley proposed the theory that short short stories are closer to poetry than to the novel and should be read like a poem, although I believe writing fiction may be a less lyrical process, correlating image not to emotion but to scene and situation and character.

Robert Shapard is editor, with James Thomas, of many of the well-known short short fiction anthologies that first helped draw attention to the genre. Their latest are *Flash Fiction Forward* (2006), *New Sudden Fiction* (2007), and, with Ray Gonzalez, *Sudden Fiction Latino* (2010), all from W. W. Norton. He has edited other anthologies as well as literary journals, such as *Manōa: A Pacific Journal of International Writing*, which he founded with Frank Stewart. He has taught at several universities, including the University of Hawaii, where he directed the writing program. His own fiction has won awards from the National Endowment for the Arts and the Council of Literary Magazines and Presses; in 2005, his collection of flash fiction, *Motel and Other Stories*, won The Predator Press's national chapbook competition.

But novels, and many conventional longer stories, are another matter. For them a prompting image may serve less as a focal point than a spur for discovering much more, as in Faulkner's *The Sound and the Fury*, which he said grew from the image of looking up at a girl in dirty underpants climbing a tree. The image is indeed there in the novel, but we might not notice it among a thousand other images if we weren't given a heads-up by CliffsNotes.

Trouble may come for the flash writer when the distinction between image-as-focus and image-as-spur gets blurred, especially if the writer was trained in workshops, as I was, to write traditional, longer stories using the methods of novelistic fiction. That is, creating a realistic world by inventing vivid detail and particulars of time and place, gesture and speech, and, especially, complex people, because it's through these people, their values, that the significance of the story comes. We can't know in advance every detail we must invent, so even if we begin with a strong idea of where we want to go, there will be the element of discovery. The goal is open-ended, finding the true story we didn't know we wanted to write. A lot of great fiction has come from this. But it was a wrong turn for me when I first tried writing flashes.

I had discovered flashes and other very short fictions in little magazines around the country during the early eighties, having just become an editor of such a magazine myself. I grew up with novels and poetry, and was in the PhD writing program in Utah, but had never seen anything like these. Were they stories? Prose poems? Something else altogether? I was entranced by their power (to suggest so much in a page or two), their beauty and their mess (some were dazzling, some were junk), and the heady feeling of freedom I got from their experiments. I copied some to take to an off-campus workshop at my friend James Thomas's house, where I asked, *What exactly are these things?* I didn't know James had discovered them, too, and was using them in teaching his university classes. With mutual enthusiasm we began to gather our favorites into an anthology we called *Sudden Fiction*, which a few years later spun off the first *Flash Fiction* anthology. But before this, what started it all for me was my wanting to write flashes, and failing.

The reason for my failure had to do with a fundamental difference, besides length, between long and short fiction, which took awhile for me to understand—no thanks to critics who, if they noticed flash fictions at all, dismissed them as fragments. The same critics implied that larger, traditional short stories were failed novels, with off-hand statements like, "There's not enough room in a short story to develop character." How easily they relegated the art of Borges, Chekhov, and Flannery O'Connor to a lesser status. I felt as if I were on an ocean voyage with only one story to read—a novel. Of course we'd want something long if it were the nineteenth century, when it took two weeks to sail from Liverpool to Boston. Yet length alone wouldn't keep us interested. What must a novel do to earn its keep? Page after page of description would put us to sleep. Too much philosophy could do the same (if we'd wanted such discourse we'd have brought a proper treatise). We need action, yes, that could thrill us, but even that can bore us—see how quickly they cut from the chase to the commercial on TV. It's people that interest us most, people making moral choices that lead them to triumph and trouble that changes their lives, and ultimately themselves. In other words, character development is a *requirement* of the novel.

But not a requirement of all fiction. The truth of this, when I saw it, exhilarated me. Wasn't it obvious? The best flashes achieved depth of vision and human significance without ever wanting to be novels. Even if they used traditional elements, they arrived at less traditional destinations. In my own flashes, I had been getting lost or sidetracked in the minutiae of realistic detail needed to develop characters. Now I saw that my goal, my focus, could be anything I wanted. Then what *should* it be? I didn't know. I tried writing flashes that culminated in clever paradoxes, or twists, or dramatic actions, but they all seemed thin. Simple images had more appeal for me, yet when I tried to see deeper into them, most of them evaporated. One, however, kept coming back to me. I don't know why it was more insistent than the others.

It was a Mexican pickup truck, overturned in the dust by the side of a highway. Like a lot of Mexican pickups, it had curtains painted inside at the top of the windshield. I decided to make it the focus of a story of no more than two or three pages.

I began by inventing characters and a minimal situation with realistic description, just as I would for a longer story. The more difficult part was knowing when to let these inventions lead me on and when not to. The truck reminded me of road trips with my family when I was a kid in New England. From those I drew details that helped establish the feel of being in a car on the highway, like the thermos cap we drank from and the embers of my parents' cigarettes at night. But other memories conjured old family issues with no end in sight. I ended up cutting most and started the story over in Mexico because it was closer to the image. I changed the characters of my parents. I changed the narrator to someone not myself. When these three people encountered the image it became clear they would have an important decision to make, and this helped me select further details. With each draft I was surer of what to keep—a line of dialogue, a gesture—and what to drop. In the last draft I cut out the painted curtains from the truck window. I had decided they were distracting and unnecessary. But then I put them back in, because they were part of the original image—this is what I mean by staying true to the image. Not until a year after the story was published and I read it again did I finally understand the importance of that detail and was glad I kept it. Actually, the pickup truck itself didn't make it to the end of the story, not the way I originally intended, yet it's still very much present—you'll see what I mean. The story, "Tamazunchale," appears below.

After this story was published I began writing other flashes by focusing on an image. In fact, as various and unformulaic as the stories in my recent chapbook of short shorts are, all of them were written using this same basic method. Has writing flashes become easy for me now? No. Every flash presents its own challenges, but my confidence has grown and I have a better feel for which focal images will work best. Is the method limited to writing flashes? No. I've used it successfully in longer works. There's no reason you can't explore a focal image in writing a flash, then use the same image again later. Many a famous novel, such as James Joyce's *Ulysses,* first took form as a short story. Images, like ideas, are renewable resources.

A FLASH FICTION PROMPT

Find an image that has a strong appeal or resonance for you and use it as the focus in writing your story. The image may be simple or complex, involving senses other than the visual, such as the spoken word, and it may come from anywhere—your personal experience (real or imagined), a film, or a magazine. The main thing is to choose an image not because you think others will like it but because somehow it matters to you. Try to use the image at the climax or at the very end of the story.

A STORY EXAMPLE

Tamazunchale

The highway had turned tropical and potholed, two narrow lanes and narrower bridges, with butterflies spattering the grillscreen we bought on good advice at the border.

My mother said, "We're on the wrong road." The map was flapping and her hair, still blond then, was flaying, air thudding through the open windows of the Buick. "We're lost."

My father sang "On the Road to Mandalay." Years later my mother said he was sometimes a stranger, after the war, although he never seemed strange to me. He had been in combat both in Europe and the Pacific, but he rarely spoke of it. He worked for an oil company, and we moved often. I was only ten at the time of our vacation, and he died when I was sixteen.

The small patch of tropics, which were not shown on my mother's map but through which we had been traveling, soon thinned out as we climbed into the desert mountains. We followed a big, backfiring diesel which we couldn't pass, and drowsing in the back of the car in the heat and swaying I could tell from the backfires when the diesel was leaving us farther behind, downhill, or uphill was coming closer again. My father spoke enthusiastically about the great city we were going to, Mexico City, high above everything, ancient and beautiful. Nothing ever changed there. My mother, so practical, consulted guidebooks by the dozen and wrote itineraries. I remember mostly rain and traffic jams.

It was hot and growing dusky when a village appeared below us. Later we found it on the map: Tamazunchale, which my mother pronounced "Thomas and Charlie," a few whitewashed houses in a dusty bend, treetops shimmering in the last of the sun. Ahead of us the diesel was plummeting toward a one-lane bridge, and around the curve on the other side of the village a small green pickup suddenly appeared, flashing its headlights. But the diesel barreled onto the bridge at top speed, not trying to slow at all, so that the pickup, in order to avoid disaster, was forced into a skid on the village side. It flipped and rolled, and as the diesel shot past, the pickup slammed finally onto its side in a wave of dust and gravel.

"God, oh God." We followed slowly downhill in the Buick. When we crossed the bridge, the dust swallowed us, then as it cleared on the other side we saw the underside of the pickup. Some villagers had already reached it. Others were still running, village women with their skirts clutched up, crying. There was a strong smell of Pemex gasoline and around one of the tires was a pale flame. One of the men, wearing white campesino pants but barechested, stretched down into the skyward window, while others held his ankles, and fetched up a howling infant.

"We've got to stop," my mother said.

Probably there was a farm family in the pickup, which had pink and green tassels and curtains painted on the inside of the windshield, a decoration common to many Mexican trucks. We had slowed almost to a stop, but not entirely. We were going on.

"They need help," my mother said.

"They've got help," my father said.

"We could take them to a hospital," my mother said.

"They'll call for help," my father said.

I watched through the rear window, the villagers crowding around. There were streaks of black in the dust cloud, but never an explosion. The cloud billowed, huge and serene.

"But what if there's no telephone?" my mother said. "How will they call for help?"

The diesel must have continued up the mountain. It had not stopped to render aid. It was nowhere in sight.

"You don't know what could happen," my father said. "You don't understand, do you?"

My mother was not a hysterical woman. If there were shouts and tears I don't remember them. If she had doubts, as she always did, about everything in her life, she took refuge in my father's direction. She never remarried.

"They'll think it's our fault," she said reasonably. "They'll come after us. They'll throw us in jail."

My father began to sing "On the Road to Mandalay."

My mother's map flapped furiously. Later she gave him some water from the cap of the big thermos she kept at her feet. When we traveled nights, there were always the embers of the cigarettes they passed between them.

I watched all the way to the top of the mountain. In the evening light, rising above the village, the dust was like a pink bomb blast: a great, unfolding flower. I understood only that my mother and father were lost.

—Robert Shapard, from Motel and Other Stories

Cornelia Parker, *Hanging Fire (Suspected Arson)*, 1999. Photo credit: Charles Meyer. From the Collection of the Institute of Contemporary Art/Boston, gift of Barbara Lee.

Stace Budzko

HANGING FIRE
A Meta-Narrative on Flash Fiction

Recently suspended Mecca Rodriguez comes right out with the definition of the day.

She goes, It's like when I'm out banging with my goonies.

And what Mecca and the rest of Frederick Douglass High are offering is their take on *What is flash fiction?* For creative inspiration we circle, as a group, Cornelia Parker's suspended sculpture *Hanging Fire (Suspected Arson)* inside the Institute of Contemporary Art (ICA) in Boston. In journals, we note what we see as well as what we *don't* see (the arsonist, the people who lived here, the words associated with such a happening). We make character sketches. We interview. We rage and rant, burn and howl.

Go on, Mecca, I say. Tell us more.

It's like when everyone's about to trip, she says.

And? I ask, hoping further details will come together, in the same way the shapes and sizes of this burnt wood somehow do, to represent the delicate blur of imagination and invention—a fiction.

And what? That's my story, fool.

The class buckles under the weight of their terrific laughter.

Unlike me, her peers seem to have a far greater understanding of what

Stace Budzko has recently been anthologized and/or published in *Flash Fiction Forward* (2006), *Brevity & Echo* (2006), *Hacks* (2007), *Quick Fiction, SmokeLong Quarterly, Long Story Short, Southeast Review, Diner, Passages North, Carve Magazine,* and Grub Street's *Free Press* (which first published a shorter version of this essay). In addition, he was a finalist for the Waasmode Short Fiction Prize, *Glimmer Train's* Very Short Fiction Award, *Night Train's* Richard Yates Short Story Award, *Carve Magazine's* Raymond Carver Short Story Award, and *Southeast Review's* World's Best Short-Short Story. A native of Maine, he received an MFA in Creative Writing at Emerson College. At present, he is a writing instructor at Emmanuel College and Grub Street as well as writer-in-residence at the Institute of Contemporary Art–Boston.

Mecca is talking about. They have, I suspect, been witness to this type of scene before. Or worse.

What Mecca is saying is *it's about the moment—a flashpoint.*

That, and a good old-fashioned gang fight.

Eventually, others let loose with their brave and complicated fictional lives.

When I was 11, I wanted to be blind. It seemed this was the missing piece between me and musical greatness. Having spent countless hours on my father's yard sale organ trying to play along with Stevie Wonder records, I was convinced *it had to be the glasses*. That's why my family would beg me to stop after the first bars of "Higher Ground."

Of course, wearing my older brother's Ray-Bans didn't pan out.

Unfortunately, playing with the lights off proved fruitless as well.

But relying on the same logic that nearly got me electrocuted when I attempted to swim underwater in the ocean with an ordinary flashlight, I took to closing my eyes—all the time. As I figured, maybe living in constant darkness like Stevie was the trick.

Oh, how I was wrong.

And after a tremendous tumble down the stairs, the dream died.

Fast forward to the present. I find myself in a contemporary art museum teaching creative writing to a group of inner-city high school students who, by their own admission, have neither stepped foot inside such a puzzling space nor have even heard the words *flash* and *fiction* spoken side by side. If confusion is the face of panic and terror, we are a dead giveaway.

The problem is inspiration. I am unable to show them how to find a story.

It was only after failing to get these frustrated yet willing scribes to set pen to paper that I would put into practice a critical lesson I learned from my attempt to be the next Motown star. And it was something I was already focused on as a fiction writer—the idea of examining the world up close, from each angle, in every light. By feeling my way around our house in those lightless moments, I eventually came to notice what I wasn't *seeing*.

As writer-in-residence at the ICA, my job is to work with Dorchester, Roxbury, and South Boston teenagers on the museum's WallTalk program. Its aim is to create exhibition-inspired narratives (fiction, poetry, drama, personal essay) in response to the art of our time. Audacious? Hopefully. And in the elusive spirit of flash fiction, our hours together in the gallery are terrifying and beautiful and not always fully appreciated at first read. Much like Frederick Douglass High's own twitchy goth specter that is student Shane Daly, who threatens to use a Zippo on his #2 pencil to start his own art project if he doesn't get his chow on, and soon.

Shortly, others begin to voice like-mindedness.

How long does it have to be? they chorus. We don't have all day, yo.

Either hungry or confused or merely restless, it's apparent time is of the essence—literally and narratively. These young authors want what they want and they want it now. It is in this *urgency* that a flash best operates. If the desire to express the feeling of being alive cannot be afforded a lengthy dramatic arc, the necessity to create a narrative as daring and troubled as a two-minute punk rock song is critical. Think The Ramones' "Blitzkrieg Bop" and you get the picture.

Scribes, I say. By definition *flash fiction has to be brief, yet intimate.*

How so? Shane asks.

We're in the punch-in-the-gut business, comrade. Offer the reader that feeling in a page or two or three or four and you just might satisfy the nonbeliever.

I point to Parker's installation for evidence.

Why write about a house's or a church's history when our story lies in its burning?

Hearing this, Shane pockets his lighter. In a rare show of vulnerability he seizes the opportunity to describe how he had to take his family's rottweiler to the vet to be put down. He reveals the instant the vet stuck the first needle into his beloved Daisy, and how quickly the dog collapsed in his arms.

Didn't take long, did it, I say.

I carried her home in a blanket, he says. I could write about that in *less* than a page.

Now we're talking, I say.

Suddenly aware of his openness, Shane retreats to the shelter of his leather trench coat.

Let's not forget, I say. This writer brings up a point when he says his story is going to break hearts in under a page. This is attitude. *Be defiant. Be daring. Be careful with words.*

From across the gallery, Dominic D'Amore shares his thoughts on wasting his time to learn any of this. Into the pages of his *Tom Sawyer* paperback, he curses.

Well said, Dom, I say. But keep in mind what your man Twain said: *The difference between the right word and the almost-right word is the difference between the lightning and the lightning bug.*

He shrugs. The others are a hard read as well. Pencils tap; text messages are sent. Sadly, we are at a tragic impasse.

Is this the mystery of flash fiction? I wonder. *Is language where we writers part ways?*

To the rescue, Angela Pierce—my new word for gutsy and wallflower— gutflower.

She peeps, Words kill.

The class erupts in outdoor voices.

Angela, I say. I like how you roll.

For the next half hour we get down to the business of writing our flash fictions. Outside, the sound of a jet engine passing overhead is a reminder of passengers taking off to near and far places. So, too, are the buses, trains, and subways of South Station that will take these kids back to school. As writers, this is what we are competing with—the constant need to move. This is strong advice for any storyteller. *Get on with it.*

But maybe it's the way the light surfs across the jagged remains of a suspected arson that holds these young writers' attention, stimulates their imagination. Or maybe it's writing to get to the end if only to stuff your pie hole. Who knows?

In a perfect world I'd like to think the students of Frederick Douglass, like those of us who bother to create anything, are tapped into photographer Walker Evans's plea: *Stare. It is the way to educate your eye, and more. Stare. Pry. Listen. Eavesdrop. . . . You are not here long.*

Before leaving, we have time to read a story or two. No takers.

Although I expect to hear from Mecca, she points to Tanya Powell, her best friend.

You have to hear this, she says.

What do you say, Tanya? I ask. Want to give it a shot?

She balks, then accepts.

We listen to Tanya describe, in her story "Goodbyes Are for Suckers," the conflicting emotions a teenager experiences just before she forever leaves her family in the Dominican Republic to go to school in Boston, a city she only knows from pictures. What she sees are passengers in their seats, the tarmac outside her window, and so on. What she doesn't see are her family members inside the terminal as well as the home she is leaving and the unexpected feelings that overtake her.

Mecca zones in on me. She winks.

When Tanya finishes with the word *ache*, I second-guess all my ideas about love.

✐

A FLASH FICTION EXERCISE

Tell It Backward

My sister was a runaway. As you can imagine, this event affected our family greatly. And each of us dealt with it in our own way. For me, I found myself asking the same question—*Where is she?* With my father it was—*How did it come to this?* Sadly, I don't believe he ever did reach the answer.

It was while teaching a short short class at Grub Street in Boston years later that I would begin to put his question to story. It was by happy accident, really. Once again a writer turned in a narrative involving a gun. And although I grew up in a house with rifles, I became increasingly frustrated when one would appear in a workshop story. What it came down to was how much weight was given to it when it was being fired, which was typically at the end. But instead of having us focus our attention here, I echoed my father, pointing out the observation that our character had first made a decision to pick up the gun. That's the moment in question, I argued, when our characters have a choice. We need to write to that point. *Let's tell it backward.*

The Exercise

In order to fully understand and appreciate characters in conflict, sometimes we have to push REWIND. Write a story that begins at the end of the action and moves backward. What was the flashpoint that initiated the event? What insights or observations did the characters initially have? How might their lives have changed if they went in another direction? One thousand words or less.

A STORY EXAMPLE

Afterthought, Aftermath, Aftershock

The next afternoon, they said the house was cool. Jill was accompanied by a nervous young man from the Fire Department, "just in case." She had him hold an extra black trash bag as she picked her way down the hall in borrowed boots. She stuffed clothes and shoes from the kids' bureau into one bag, miscellany from her closet into the other. They could sort out which ones were too water-damaged later. The fire hadn't gotten this far, but the walls were smoke and water-stained anyway. Into a third bag, she swept everything from her desk—photographs, papers, jewelry. The other end of the house—kitchen and family room, where the fire had started—was a loss.

The fireman (or was it fire*boy*) deposited her on the sidewalk, where she sat down on the curb to wait for her ride. Jill's aunt Nancy had taken the kids to the park, she'd be by soon. Part of her wailed, *We dodged foreclosure, and now THIS?* Running her hands through her hair, Jill went through the list of things she needed to do: Call the insurance company again, make a withdrawal from the bank, sort through their clothes, start looking for somewhere to stay, call the children's father.

The night before, Jill hadn't waited to ask herself why she was awake before her feet hit the carpeting. When she finally made the connection—smoke, smoke necessitated fire—she didn't bother to find her slippers or a jacket. She pounded across the hall to the kids' room, and even though the day before she'd sworn Don was too heavy for her to carry anymore, had him scooped up and draped over her shoulder before he was awake. When he did wake, he only whined, "What's going on?" With Jessica on her other hip, all she could say was, "Hold on to me, honey, hold on."

The fire was already eating the doorway from the kitchen to the family room. Jill went straight for the door. There was a moment of fumbling with the knob when she almost dropped Don. He clutched her—monkey-like, arms and legs at the same time.

Then they were out.

Jill made it to the sidewalk before the combination of crying kid and toddler mixed with release hit her and she sank to the pavement. In the minutes before the fire brigade arrived, she remained blinkless to the sky above the streetlights. It seemed immeasurable, dark, and safe.

—Anna Geneva Renz, student

Robert Olen Butler

A SHORT SHORT THEORY

To be brief, it is a short short story and not a prose poem because it has at its center a character who yearns.

Fiction is a temporal art form. Poetry can choose to ignore the passage of time, for there is a clear sense of a poem being an *object*, composed densely of words, existing in space. This is true even when the length of the line is not an objectifying part of the form, as in a prose poem. And a poem need not overtly concern itself with a human subject. But when you have a human being centrally present in a literary work and you let the line length run on and you turn the page, you are, as they say in a long storytelling tradition, "upon a time." And as any Buddhist will tell you, a human being (or a "character") cannot exist for even a few seconds of time on planet Earth without desiring something. *Yearning* for something, a word I prefer because it suggests the deepest level of desire, where literature strives to go. Fiction is the art form of human yearning, no matter how long or short that work of fiction is.

James Joyce spoke of a crucial characteristic of the literary art form, something he called the *epiphany*, a term he appropriated from the

One of America's foremost literary writers, **Robert Olen Butler** was born near St. Louis. His many works include the Pulitzer Prize–winning *A Good Scent from a Strange Mountain* (1992). Known for his willingness to take chances with form, Butler's most recent exploration of the short short story led to *Intercourse* (2008); in "crystalline prose," as *Publishers Weekly* describes, 100 stories voice the deep inner monologues of 50 couples. This collection follows *Severance* (2006), stories of exactly 240 words that represent the mind's final internal monologue at the moment of death by beheading. *Hell* (novel, 2009) uses imbedded short short stories as a narrative strategy. He teaches at Florida State University. His book of lectures on the creative process (*From Where You Dream*, 2005, edited by Janet Burroway) is widely used in creative writing courses.

Catholic Church meaning, literally, "a shining forth." The Church uses it to describe the shining forth of the divinity of the baby Jesus. The word made flesh. In literary art, the flesh is made word. And Joyce suggests that a work of fiction moves to a moment at the end where something about the human condition shines forth in its essence.

I agree. But I also believe that all good fiction has two epiphanies. There is the one Joyce describes, and there is an earlier epiphany, very near the beginning of a story (or a novel), when the yearning of the character shines forth. This does not happen in explanatory terms but rather is a result of the presence of that yearning in all the tiny, sense-driven, organically resonant moments in the fiction, the accumulation of which reaches a critical mass which then produces that shining forth.

And because of the extreme brevity of the short short story, these two epiphanies often—even typically—occur at the same moment. The final epiphany of a literary short short is also the shining forth of the character's yearning.

It has been traditional to think that a story has to have a "plot" while a poem does not. Plot, in fact, is yearning challenged and thwarted. A short short story, in its brevity, may not have a fully developed plot, but it must have the essence of a plot, yearning.

A FLASH FICTION EXERCISE

Write a story that depicts two characters who are both yearning for something. They should be in a relationship—romantic, familial, social—and their needs should be in opposition to each other, or should be challenged and thwarted, one by the other. Create background events that provide a foil to the characters' inner desires, further layering your plot. (In the following example, the event is 9/11.)

A STORY EXAMPLE

Kevin Smith, 32, advertising copywriter
Julia Hanson Smith, 30, graphic designer
in their apartment in Brooklyn, the night of September 11, 2001

Kevin

I know the night is filled with smoke and with fire and I would not have thought it would be my wife clinging to me now because of what I have done: I should have gone out the door last night after my clumsiness, she was half-turned at the stove, the steam rising before her from the boiling rice, and all that I'd planned carefully to say came out impulsively, simply, badly, *I am in love* and she knew it was not her and she laid the lid on the pot and she turned her back to me and later we sat in chairs in the dark of our living room for a long while, the pot charred black on the stove, and I did not go and then it was this morning and then the long day and I am in love and I think it is not with her, but tonight, in this moment, we dare not change a thing

Julia

how can it be so quiet from across the river, if you do not make yourself look you might never realize the terrible thing going on, and he and I do not look, we know but we choose for this night not to look, even into our own hearts, though I can hear faintly through the wall someone weeping and from another place the murmur of television voices, and I see myself standing in an open window high above the city: I cannot go back inside and I cannot step into the empty air, and from this distance I am only a figure standing in a window, I can only try to imagine what I am feeling

—Robert Olen Butler, from *Intercourse*

Steve Almond

GETTING THE LEAD OUT
How Writing Really Bad Poetry
Yields Really Better Short Stories

What happened was I just got tired of prose. I got tired of the slow, cautious accretion of detail. The flabby piles of words. The self-conscious sense of intention that plagues traditional prose storytelling. Oh, the metaphors. The symbols. The blocking of each scene, what poet Lynn Emanuel (God bless her) calls the "horror: getting Raoul into the elevator." How dreary it all felt, which is what happens when you suck as a prose writer.

So I stopped cold turkey and started writing poems instead. For a year, I wrote nothing but poems. I don't have to tell you that those sucked, too. I thought they were sly, heartbreaking, *deep*. None of my friends had the heart to tell me otherwise, and I didn't have many friends anyway, because I was a poet, appropriately bereaved and full of the hot misery of my calling. I went to poetry readings night after night and burned with passionate anxiety. I was in my thirties, living alone, desperate for water and miles from the nearest fountain.

On and on I went. Oh God. Hundreds of poems. Thousands. It was like some diseased second adolescence had taken hold of my innards—the heart and spleen in particular—and wrung till dry. To ask what I wrote poems about is somewhat missing the point. What *didn't* I write poems about? Nothing was sacred because everything was sacred in my fren-

Steve Almond burst onto the literary scene with his controversial and widely acclaimed short story collection *My Life in Heavy Metal* (2002). His work is known for its conversational style and brutal honesty—especially in the exploration of sociological and sexual interactions—and for his ability to provide uncanny depth in very short spaces. His success continued with the popular nonfiction book *Candyfreak* (2004), then with a second short story collection, *The Evil B.B. Chow* (2005), and an epistolary novel, *Which Brings Me to You* (co-written with Julianna Baggott, 2006). His newest book is a collection of essays, *Not That You Asked* (2007). Born in New Haven, Connecticut, Almond now lives outside Boston with his wife and his daughter, Josephine. His online home is www.stevenalmond.com.

zied condition, every burp and dribble I witnessed or expelled. Homeless people, chicken fat, Sir Edmund Hillary, frightening insects, broken toilets, winter smokers, spring finches, unsuspecting landscapes, women who wouldn't sleep with me (there were a lot), women who would sleep with me (there were two), women who slept with me then screwed me over (uh, two), parents who had never loved me sufficiently, brothers who had bullied me, friends who had done me wrong, a blooming list of enemies, paranoia, ambition, nightmares, giardia, unfriendly cashiers, old crushes, politicians, and the demolition of the Boston Garden. That's a week's worth right there.

How was I able to sustain such output? It helped that my standards were appallingly low. But there was something else going on, something less narcissistically corrupt. I wasn't editing myself. At least in terms of my ideas or the path they took. I wasn't trying to construct a "larger narrative." I was interested in sudden impact, and thus dispensed with the logistics and throat-clearing that had come to represent such a large percentage of my prose (best guess: 87 percent).

This led to a compression of sensual and psychological detail, or what might be referred to, flatteringly, as flights into the lyric register. The problem—and it wasn't a problem in the end—was that I wasn't a poet. I was a storyteller. No matter how hard I tried, I couldn't undo my desire to move a character through dangerous terrain. I didn't have the knack for true abstraction, pure thought, authentic associations.

And so eventually it was impressed upon me by someone with enough authority to silence my ego that I wasn't writing poems, but extremely short short stories and essays. It took me another few years to admit this to myself, and still longer to stitch together all my cheesily enjambed lines. But the evidence presented itself and I was tired enough, for once, not to object.

So that's what happened: I abandoned the orthodoxies of prose and indulged in certain poetic excesses and thereby got the lead out. There are worse creation stories, I imagine. In any event, creation stories don't matter. Creation does. That which feels dead under the fingertips must be made to feel alive. It's okay to hurry if you're not dodging the truth. We haven't all that much time, anyway.

_⁓_

A FLASH FICTION EXERCISE

Stop whatever story you're working on and convert the whole thing into a poem. This will be a much shorter piece, in which you bid various extra words and characters and subplots goodbye. (There is no need to wave to them.) Don't worry about whether your poem is any good. Just make your decisions as honestly as you can. Once finished you may, at your discretion, remove the line breaks and examine the resulting piece of prose.

Stop

Or maybe you're here, in Sturbridge, Mass.,
off the pike, punching the register, Roy Rogers,
a girl in a brown smock. America comes at you on buses,
in caps and shorts, fuming. What the hell,
you're killing each other, anyway.
This kind of loneliness. What are words?
You've got chores, duties,
an inanimate world that needs you.
Sometimes, late afternoon, you scrape the grill
and figure: this could be love, this clean violence,
the meaty shavings and steel beneath.
There are other ideas out there, in magazines
and movies, sweaters, perfume, your beautiful money.
But you see your life, that which persists,
the dumpster out back, the counter dulled
by your hands, relish troughs to fill.
Some days the clouds are so thick they seem weighted.
You are kind and not especially pretty.
You do your job. You are polite. At great expense,
you smile. Your best friend died
just down the road, in an accident at night.
You laid a pink bear before the marker
and you persisted, you persist.

A STORY EXAMPLE

Stop

Or maybe you're here, in Sturbridge, Mass., off the pike, punching
the register, Roy Rogers, a girl in a brown smock. America comes
at you on buses, in caps and shorts, fuming. What the hell, you're
killing each other, anyway. This kind of loneliness. What are words?
You've got chores, duties, an inanimate world that needs you.
Sometimes, late afternoon, you scrape the grill and figure: this could
be love, this clean violence, the meaty shavings and steel beneath.
There are other ideas out there, in magazines and movies, sweaters,
perfume, bales of beautiful money. But you see your life, that which
persists, the dumpster out back, the counter dulled by your hands,
relish troughs to fill. Some days the clouds are so thick they seem
weighted. You are kind and not especially pretty. You do your job.
You are polite. At great expense, you smile. Your best friend died just
down the road, in an accident at night. You laid a pink bear before
the marker and you persisted, you persist.

—Steve Almond, story from *The Sun*

Kim Chinquee

FLASH FICTION, PROSE POETRY, AND MEN JUMPING OUT OF WINDOWS
Searching for Plot and Finding Definitions

Plot: the sequence or progress of events in a play, novel, film, etc. (*American Century Dictionary*, 1995).

Is it essential in flash fiction? I can only stress the importance of plot in any literary genre. And though flash fiction is its own little devil, getting away with bending many rules, this genre is not excused from plot. In many cases, the sequence of events in a particular flash may be difficult to distinguish; likely, in flash fiction, plot is often presented in nontraditional ways, arising through other elements necessary to make a successful literary story—character, language, point of view, setting, structure, voice, each element can be accountable for plot. Plot in flash is inclusive and exclusive. For example, rhythmic language in a piece can suggest playfulness, and juxtaposed with some eccentric detail, the combination of these elements here can make a good flash fiction. Deadpan tones of horrifying accounts can justify a plot line. A third-person flash ending in first person can twist a piece and thus render it successful. Providing descriptive elements and omitting the events can also work. When used effectively, omission of details can gear a plot. Plot is vital in flash fiction, propelling it to its brevity.

Kim Chinquee is author of the flash fiction/prose poetry collection *OH BABY* (2008), the forthcoming flash fiction/prose poetry collection *Pretty* (2010), and is co-editor of the anthology *Online Writing: The Best of the First Ten Years* (2009). Chinquee grew up in Wisconsin, and served in the air force as a medical technician. Her flash skills were honed while pursuing an MA at the University of Southern Mississippi and an MFA at the University of Illinois; her work has appeared widely in such journals as *Noon, Conjunctions, Denver Quarterly, Quick Fiction, Notre Dame Review, Mississippi Review, New Orleans Review, Willow Springs, Fiction*, and she has quickly grown to prominence in the fields of flash and prose poetry. Chinquee is the recipient of a Henfield and a Pushcart Prize. She currently resides in Buffalo, New York, where she teaches creative writing.

Aristotle's *Poetics* emphasizes the importance of plot in "drama," stating, "The plot is the essential element of a tragedy. . . . The plot does not concern what has happened as an isolated incident."

So, basically, event is not the only necessity of plot; the surrounding elements procure it.

Say a man jumps out of a window. We have a major incident, though the elements surrounding that incident justify the plot: Will something catch his fall? Is he acting as a stunt man? Is the window high? On a bottom floor? What are the details of the man? His life? Does he live alone? Is he getting married? Having children? Divorced? What's his age? His livelihood? Is he homeless? What's his style?

The following are five examples, evolutions of a particular event. This case: Man Jumping Out of Window.

1. The man escaped the fire, jumping from the window, carrying his newborn. His wife was inside making brownies but he told himself he didn't care about the wife now since she was cheating with the neighbor. She knew how to put the fire out. Everyone was out now and he handed the baby over and ran back, charging in. "Sherry," he said. He ran through flames to find her.

2. A woman leaves her father alone in her apartment. He remembers his old days as a paratrooper, but he isn't old anymore, it's 1952 and he is in Korea. Out the window is the sky, the buildings below, the breeze. His back feels heavy, and he stands on the ledge and waits for the commander.

3. The man jumped out of the window. It was a big window, wide, with a broken screen, the wire bent and fractured. The ledge wasn't any different and the man, he was clean and tailored. His tie was striped, but usually it was checkered. He wasn't sure why, today, he'd chosen this one. He wasn't sure about anything. He got to work on time. He always did. He had to.

4. I like this window. I grew up here. It gets hot up here in summer, and in winter I wear coats and scarves and mittens. I can hear the cows moo. Moo, they say. They're talking. Jump, I hear them tell me.

5. No one knew why Mr. Collins jumped. He was a quiet man, friendly to the people and giving children suckers. He worked with shoes. He sold them. He lived alone and had a bunny named Kip that hopped around in his apartment. He went to church and sat at the same pew every Sunday, singing hymns and praying for forgiveness.

In essence, the basic event is present in each of these examples. But obviously, in each case, this single event does not "make" the story; the elements surrounding the "event" become the guts, all entwined together. Story #1 becomes not only the story of a man jumping from a window, but the story of a newborn, the man suspecting infidelity, and then his conscience being compounded with a life-threatening situation and his own guilt. Story #2 complicates the event by the fact that this man has dementia. Story #3 seems to be about a man with suicidal intentions, but the omission of certain details may leave the reader wondering if this is indeed the case. Story #4 is in first person, with an unreliable narrator of an uncertain age who hears voices. Story #5 involves a more omniscient and distant narrator, speculating about the nature of Mr. Collins's intentions.

In these shorter pieces, in flash, one element can monopolize, yet generally, elements may become more blurred than in a traditional short story; here, more likely another element makes itself the plot, so to speak. In Story #4, for example, the distant first-person narration indicates an emotional detachment, and the narrator saying that the cows tell him to jump reveals some delusion, and the combination of these factors further lend to plot.

If this becomes the case, if a flash can become a piece that focuses on language, setting, or character, for instance, why not call these pieces prose poems? The discussion of the differences/similarities and origins of flash fiction and prose poetry is extensive, and this account will hardly skim the surface of these studies. However, I will say this: prose poems can be flashes and flashes can be prose poems. They are interchangeable. They are more inclusive than exclusive—each, of the other. Quite simply, the more the elements of these genres become blurred, the harder it is to distinguish whether the piece is more prose poem than flash. If only pieces were color-coded; a concrete flash could be black and a solid prose poem white (or vice versa), but most prose poems and flashes would then become gray, some darker/lighter than others. However, that distinction could also depend on the observer's eyes, the timing and mood, the light of that one moment. It would be easier if it were about biology, with dominant and recessive genes, each piece mapped out on a chart; but then, what would be the control? The median, the standard deviation? It begins to lean toward science, or math, away from those elements that make language so affecting.

With all that put aside, in simple general terms, I believe that a prose poem is more about language and poetics, whereas a flash carries more narrative and story.

Michael Benedikt's introduction in *The Prose Poem: An International Anthology*, published in 1976, provides a prose poem definition. He answers the following question: "What are the special properties of the prose poem as they appear today?" He basically lists them as: (1) the unconscious, (2) the use of everyday speech, (3) a visionary thrust, (4) a certain humor, and (5) a hopeful skepticism (48–50).

The unconscious speaks to the absence of the line break, thus allowing each word more equal weight; unlike "regular" poetry, a poem does not single out individual words simply because that word completes a line or stanza, surrounded by its white space. Furthermore, everyday speech stems from that unconscious; Benedikt reiterates Levi-Strauss and Chomsky's theory that reality derives from one's language, which allows for that visionary thrust. He continues, stating that humor and wit can tie into the moral of a piece (as in the work of James Tate and Russell Edson), and can even be taken to absurd extremes, which tie into hopeful skepticism. Benedikt does not speak of plot here, nor does he emphasize a plot line. He stays specific, focused on the prose poem, the language and flavor of the contents.

He includes works that incorporate some or all of the above elements. "Antique I" by legendary prose poet Arthur Rimbaud (1854–91), for instance, involves all of these, and although it is unfair and perhaps impossible to label each line exclusively, I believe that some lines (and words) provide more evidence of Benedikt's definition than others. In my attempt to dissect Rimbaud's piece, I concluded that the opening introduces a certain humor: "Grateful son of Pan! Beneath your brow crowned with sprays of flowers and berries, roll your eyes, those precious circumferences." "Your heart beats in your belly, where the double sex sleeps," reveals absurdity. And with hopeful skepticism the story ends: "Walk off, through the night, gently moving that thigh, that second thigh; and then, this whole left leg" (95). Clearly, the visionary thrust is present in this piece.

The term "flash fiction" doesn't have the lengthy history of the term "prose poem," which originated in the 1860s, thanks to Baudelaire. James Thomas, Denise Thomas, and Tom Hazuka, in their 1992 anthology *Flash Fiction*, were the first to define flash fiction as a story of about 750 words, or a story that could fit onto two facing pages of a typical digest-size literary magazine; a story that is likely to include all those same elements of longer fiction, such as point-of-view, character, voice, setting, structure, and so on.

The flash fiction definitions I've seen have also included all elements of fiction, and flash is distinguished from short stories also by length. In my research regarding prose poems, I have not seen a prose poem defined by length, only by specific elements included within text.

How, then, can one arrive at a concrete way of distinguishing flash fiction from prose poetry? If looking for specifics, like whether a piece has more flash tendencies or more sightings of a prose poem, one could write many interesting dissertations on this topic, charting out and color-coding the black or gray or white. But all-in-all, they are simply interchangeable. Each can be the other. They exist, and that's what is most important. So I recommend getting out the pen (or getting to the computer). Start with a purple sun, or a man climbing in a window, and write. And then see where it takes you.

A FLASH FICTION EXERCISE

Pick an event with one main character (for instance: a man jumps from a window, or a man runs through flames to find his wife, or a woman trips over her shoe on the way to the bus, or a girl chokes on a walnut, or a baby gets a bee sting, and so on). Write five different flashes, each using the same event, but vary the voice and tone, characters and settings.

After you have your five pieces, study the characters, settings, points-of-view, structure, tones, and voices. The order of events. Compare, take note, and study again. See what's working, and change what's not.

In the story example below, author Diane Williams goes so far as to name the plot in the third paragraph: "Here's the plot: When the baby was stung, at first no one was sure what happened, but then the mother said, 'His arm is getting all pink.'" But is that the plot? How does this announcement enhance the plot further? The answer: it leads the reader to that powerful last sentence.

A STORY EXAMPLE

Naaa

There's the baby who gets the bee sting. In my opinion, there's the baby carrying around a paperweight that, if he had dropped it on his bare foot, would or could have broken his foot.

The mother of the babies has sprained her ankle, and chipped a bone in it, and she is using a cane to help her get around.

Here's where the plot is thickening. Here's the plot: When the baby was stung, at first no one was sure what happened, but then the mother said, "His arm is getting all pink." Not to go on and on—the sting was discovered on the tip of the baby's thumb. Finally—I was there—at the moment of the discovery, when just then: the baby stopped his crying.

I was the person who took the paperweight away from the baby. He walks. He's old enough to walk, just old enough, which is why I call him a baby. He was disappointed, but did not appear outraged, when I took the paperweight away from him. "You should not be carrying this around," I said.

If this were an issue larger than worry about human extinction, I could allow myself to think about it.

Secretly, I believe the paperweight is an item which should never have existed, *ever.*

The facts of the matter are complex, but this baby's power is nowhere limited.

This baby's power is his renunciation of all power.

—Diane Williams, from *Some Sexual Success Stories
Plus Other Stories in Which God Might Choose to Appear*

Deb Olin Unferth

PUT YOURSELF IN DANGER
An Examination of Diane Williams's Courageous Short

Flash fiction is a place for reckless daring. You write strange sentences in a new voice. You attempt a bold plot structure. You explore a topic you've always avoided. But playing isn't enough—you must also take risks.

I think of flash fiction, or the short short, as being more like a painting than like long fiction. The ambition of a short short is not to make readers "lose themselves"—how far lost can you get in a couple of pages? The effect of the short is fast (even if the making of it isn't) and yet complete. The shape of the piece leaps out at the reader and is taken in as a whole, as if it were a picture.

In this sense, the short is the more intellectual of the fiction forms. It's a place for writers to talk *about* fiction and its feats in that weird mysterious way that fiction talks beyond the story on the page. The short makes us consider such questions as: What is the essential element of "story"? How much can the author leave out and still create a moving, complete narrative? If I remove all backstory, all exposition, all proper nouns, all dialogue—or if I write a story that consists only of dialogue—in what way is it still a story? What is a story?

The most satisfying way to write and read shorts is to deal with bookfuls of the things. Just a handful won't help. A successful collection of

Deb Olin Unferth is the author of the flash fiction collection *Minor Robberies* (2007) and the novel *Vacation* (2008), both from McSweeney's. *Minor Robberies* is included with two other books of short fiction, by Dave Eggers and Sarah Manguso, the complete collection of which is titled *One Hundred and Forty-Five Stories in a Small Box*. Her fiction has appeared in *Harper's*, *Conjunctions*, *NOON*, and the *Pushcart Prize* and *New Sudden Fiction* anthologies, among others. Her Napkin Fiction titled "Joke" appeared on *Esquire* online (March 5, 2008). Born in Chicago, Illinois, Unferth is assistant professor of creative writing at Wesleyan University in Connecticut.

shorts creates not only a set of stories but a worldview, a philosophy of removal and absence. It becomes a reflection of the writer's mind. You can almost see the rhythm of the writer's thoughts on the page, each story turning into a single painting in a series.

Take as an example the Diane Williams's story "Marriage and the Family" (from her collection *Excitability*, published by Dalkey Archive Press), which can be found at the end of this essay. It opens with a woman who is contemplating her local office supply shop. She describes the shop in a quirky, humorous voice: The women who run the shop all look the same, she jokes in the first paragraph. They act as if they know the narrator when really they don't, she goes on. What phonies they are. The shop is silly. It's filled with balloons and brightly colored paper.

Halfway through the piece, the voice begins to shift. "They do wear very tight pants," the narrator observes. This remark is surprising. It has a note, not of playful teasing, but of detached judgment. In the next paragraph the narrator says, "I have never had an argument with one of the sisters." Strange. Why would she have had an argument with them? The narrator then recites a long, terrifying argument that she says did *not* happen, and suddenly she is filled with rage—at the sisters, at the shop, at the entire shiny, sickly clean, suburban world of which this shop is just one white-painted participant: "You frighten me more than anyone I could ever look at."

Now the story is becoming an angry manifesto or a critical essay, and the title, "Marriage and the Family," recalls the marriage manuals for housewives of the 1950s—those practical guidebooks, once quite common, that dictated how women ought to behave in order to be the perfect housewife.

At the end of the story a man confronts her. When she had first arrived, she had done a poor parking job outside the shop, pulling in crazily as if she were in a movie with a chase on and lives at stake. She had thought of that parking job as heroic, as the one impassioned action she can take in a dead fake world. The fact that this is the act she has chosen for her courageous feat—parking—is funny, but it's also very sad. The man thinks of it as untoward, dangerous even. "I saw you out there," he says, accusingly.

Now, imagine for a moment that the man isn't talking to the narrator about her parking job. Imagine for a moment that he's talking to the author, Diane Williams, instead and that he's talking about this very story and that he says to her in that same disapproving tone, not, "I saw you out there," but, "I read what you wrote. How dare you write such a thing."

I can imagine someone saying that. The story is that reckless.

It feels as though lives are at stake, her life.

So in this short piece, we have seen: the development of a complex psychology, a set of startlingly original sentences, a sharp emotional shift from calm observation to rage, an unparalleled style, a knock-out title, a social critique, and a very moving story about one woman's private crisis while running a common errand.

I dare you to write such a thing.

A FLASH FICTION EXERCISE

In my college fiction workshops, when we discuss a story and use it as a springboard for writing, I generally give the students three separate exercises: the first is to generate *content* for a new story, the second is to have them try their hand at *style* innovations, the third is to get them thinking about *structure*. Here, I offer the following 10-minute exercises:

1. *Content exercise:* Write a story about a situation in which you felt alienated and uncomfortable.

2. *Style exercise:* Write a story that is a list of things that did *not* happen.

3. *Structure exercise:* Write a story in which a dramatic emotional shift occurs from the beginning of the story to the end.

A STORY EXAMPLE

Marriage and the Family

Every time I go in there I am thinking, This time I will get the sisters straight, which one is which. But each time I go in there I think there is a new sister, one I have never seen before, who gets me mixed up.

This new sister will act as though she knows me very well, as though I am quite familiar to her.

What is the same or almost the same about all of the sisters is this: their hair and their clothing, their faces, their jewelry, their ages, their expressions, their attitudes. I do not think they are quintuplets, if there are that many of them, or anything like that, but there is the possibility.

The sisters run a business where there are balloons around. It is a print and office supply shop in my town. It is new, and they behave as though they will be very successful, or as though they already are.

Everything is clean, such as stacks of tangerine and fuchsia paper for writing, and pens to match, which must be too expensive to buy. I wouldn't buy the pens.

Two or three of the sisters may be married. They wear tiny rectangular or round diamonds set into gold bands, and plain gold wedding bands to go with. A couple of the sisters only wear the diamonds.

There is a blond child I saw once, who looks happy and well adjusted. One of the sisters laughed and joked with the child. She hugged him and she kissed him.

A mother of a sister called in once, and she was spoken to sweetly by one of the sisters.

They do wear very tight pants. The pants hug and squeeze their bottoms so that there must be some discomfort for the sisters when they have to sit down to do their work, or even when they just stand—the pants are that tight.

I have never had an argument with one of the sisters. One of these sisters has never ridiculed me, or made me feel unwelcome, as though I were trying to take over in there, or take advantage of any of them, when I shopped there.

Not one of the sisters ever yelled at me, told me to get out of her way, or implied that I came into the shop too often and that something was suspicious.

I never yelled back at one of the sisters to say I buy a lot in her shop, and that I could just go somewhere else. I never said I have my whole life in my hands when I come in there. I never got myself into a rage. I never looked at a sister and thought, You frighten me more than anyone I could ever look at—take a look at you—and your whole attitude is wrong.

Your attitude is abysmal. Your attitude is as if you have been stung, or are stinging, or are getting ready to be bitten, or to bite.

The last time I was in the shop, this is what happened: a man was in there. I didn't know for what purpose. He looked suspicious. He didn't buy anything. He was darting around, and he was looking at me, and looking at me, until I had to pay attention to him. Then he said, "I saw you out there," meaning out in front of the shop. What he meant was, he had seen the way I had parked my car. I knew that had to be it. I had even surprised myself with the way I had done it. I had never done anything like that parking.

I was proud of myself like a hero should be proud, who risks his life, or who doesn't risk his life, but who saves somebody, *anybody!*

"You could have killed somebody!" was what that man said to me.

—Diane Williams, from Excitability

Sherrie Flick

FLASH IN A PAN
Writing Outside of Time's Boundaries

I once fancied myself a poet, so I went to college in New England, the place where the poets lived. Crumbling stone walls, roads converging in a wood. But I never got the line break, so I decided I must be a fiction writer and walked over to the "other" workshop to write stories. Beginning, middle, end. Fifteen to 36 pages.

But I still wasn't happy.

Then, one day my friend Guy placed Raymond Carver's *Fires* into my hands. Reading it was like being hit by a bolt of lightning. Yes, tiny stories—of course! Not poems but intense, concise, emotionally fraught . . . fiction. I wanted to make these things.

I did just that. My professor held one up by the corner of the page as if it were contaminated and announced to the class, "This is not a story." And so it was that I entered the life of a flash fiction writer, head-butting my way into a writing "career."

I never understood the debate about flash fiction: Is it a story; is it a poem? It isn't a poem because the author doesn't *want it* to be a poem. When a poet writes a prose poem and says, "This is a prose poem," everyone says okay and that's that. But when a flash fiction writer says, "This is a story," there's often a collective stomping of brakes on the writing high-

Sherrie Flick is the author of Flume Press's 2004 award-winning flash fiction chapbook *I Call This Flirting*. Her flash fiction has been anthologized in the major collections: *New Sudden Fiction* (2007), *Flash Fiction Forward* (2006), *Sudden Stories: The MAMMOTH Book of Miniscule Fiction* (2003), and *You Have Time for This* (2007). Flick's work is highly regarded as being "risk-taking, passionate, and original"; her layering and condensing of time is especially unique. A native of Beaver Falls, Pennsylvania, with an MA in English Literature from the University of Nebraska–Lincoln, she returned to the state to work as a freelance writer and to co-found and serve as artistic director of the Gist Street Reading Series in Pittsburgh. Her first novel, *Reconsidering Happiness*, will be published in fall 2009.

way as naysayers screech to a halt to gauge its storyness. Don't be afraid, I want to tell those naysayers. It's just a little story. Like a long story, but shorter.

One thing I love about flash fiction is the way time can be manipulated. It isn't that time *can't* be manipulated in longer stories; it's just that it can be messed with in flash fiction in ways that not only surprise you, the writer, but also surprise and satisfy the reader.

The first step is to forget about plot. I just finished writing a novel, and with a novel I had to have plot in my back pocket 24/7, or I was screwed. Be happy that you can forget about plot as you write your little story. It's freedom. By forgetting about plot you can suspend yourself in a timeless limbo. Let yourself freefall. Think about objects and details, about how they happen in real time. Focus on them. These are the things that will keep your story rooted in time while you're not thinking about plot:

> Half open door. Remember last summer? Muted light. The neighbor's Chihuahua on the loose again. That breeze. The tiny barking. I need to call Martha.

We're floating in time here, in this small paragraph of mine, but the details are specific. Time and detail are inseparable. The objects become touchstones for the reader. More important, they become guides that liberate the writer to move freely about.

Writing about what isn't true, as if it is, can help you freefall as well. Here's how my story "Oklahoma Men" (p. 124) begins: "In Oklahoma men drink their coffee black." Well, that's a generalization, right? Not really. It's a precise perspective that begins to conjure a specific (if warped) Oklahoma, suspended in time but loaded with detail.

While moving gracefully through your world of simultaneity, don't complicate your verb tense. A key to flash fiction is really, really (really) good sentences. Your sentences should be muscular—not flabby. Revise them until the last thing you notice is their structure. If you write something like: "The men in Oklahoma <u>were often seen</u> drinking their hot coffee very black," with "were often seen" in there it's harder to float around in time because you've stuck yourself in some dead-end past tense. This isn't just any perspective; it's one clear shot at it. They didn't "begin to drink" their coffee. Their coffee wasn't "very" anything. They weren't "seen." *The men drink their coffee black.* It's a statement that unfetters you as a writer. It's active. Shoot for that, and it'll pay you back with the opportunity to be complex elsewhere.

After you have your first draft and you've let yourself write your story outside of time's boundaries, take a good look at it. Get yourself a cup of tea. Let yourself think about plot just a little. Allow yourself to revise every sentence at least a dozen times. Let the meaning rise to the surface. Let yourself write about the past, present, and future all at once.

⌁

A FLASH FICTION EXERCISE
Writing a Warped Encyclopedia Entry (200–250 words)

1. Pick a state or city that interests you, that you've been to, that you can talk about in detail; but don't be so close to the place that you've lost perspective on it.

2. Make a list of details that define this place for you. Weird little details that others might not notice. The kinds of food, the kinds of people, strange local phrases, diners where locals eat, weather, rituals, something interesting that you saw when you visited. Include the smallest detail. Make things up. Put some time into this list. It will serve as source material for your story.

3. Read some old-time encyclopedia entries. Not from Wikipedia, but from the hardback books people used to sell door to door. You can find these at your library or local thrift store. Notice the intriguing, stilted tone. What qualities does this type of writing possess? Take some notes.

4. Write an encyclopedia entry of the town or state you picked in #1, mimicking the tone of an old-time encyclopedia, capturing a sense of place, but without being accurate. This is fiction, after all.

A STORY EXAMPLE

Oklahoma Men

In Oklahoma men drink their coffee black. It costs 15 cents and comes in small Styrofoam cups the color of Elmer's Glue, the color of new light bulbs.

They don't slurp or blow. The coffee remains as placid as a lake. Tea is not served.

Younger men add sugar. They do this by opening two stiff packets at once. The grains pour slowly into the dark liquid, settling like trusting pioneers in the bottom of the cups. In this way, they know something dark and sweet is always waiting.

The men sit around square tables in the early, early morning in corner cafes called Karen's or Jake's or the Bluebird. Humming fluorescent lights hum and light, while baseball hats with feed company logos reach from one pink temple to the next. Out back, big green pick-up trucks tick and settle.

When the men speak, it's in four-part harmony. They wear leather boots that creak. They eat donuts and never turn quickly on one another or brush crumbs onto the floor.

As the sun trips through the plate-glass window, they talk about how things were—how much harder everyone worked—how much harder they must work now. The men look at the front of their hands, then they look at the back. They settle in their seats like hard rubber; they push their hats back on their heads to see clearly across their days, across hills and miles, across all the fences they've strung together to know where they've been, to know how to get back to what it was they started.

—Sherrie Flick, from *I Call This Flirting*

Mark Budman

EXPOSE YOURSELF TO FLASH

When I first heard the term "flash fiction," I almost laughed. I imagined a tall man who opens his raincoat in public to show off his writing. Actually, there is nothing wrong with exposing yourself to art. To answer this higher calling is not a laughing matter. Ask Aesop, Chekhov, or Hemingway.

What is flash? No one would object if I say that flash fiction is terse by definition. But terse and concise can't be the only answers. While one can argue that, for example, the word "I" is a good story in itself (what can be more laconic and yet all-encompassing than a story of me?), most observers would say that just "I" is not enough. The reader wants the story to go on. What happens when "I" enters the scene in all his energetic glory (because flash is as energetic as a short-distance sprinter)? Does he expose himself? Does he spill his guts for the reader? Does he make the world a better or at least a more interesting place as a result?

As a reader, I want more, but not much more. I want the un-said, the un-written. A hint, an allusion, a suggestion. I want to work with the writer to help her build a world for me. I want a symbiotic relationship, a collaboration. I want something that a writer of a long work won't give me out of jealousy.

Mark Budman, born and raised in the former Soviet Union, now resides in New York state. His early fascination with the short short inspired him in 2000 to start the *Vestal Review* (with co-editor Sue O'Neill), the first online magazine devoted solely to flash fiction. He and Tom Hazuka (p. 31) co-edited the recent prize-winning flash fiction anthology *You Have Time for This* (2007) and *Best American Flash Fiction of the 21st Century* (2007). While Budman continues to lecture and teach widely on the subject of flash, his own works have appeared in such magazines as *Mississippi Review, Virginia Quarterly, Iowa Review, McSweeney's, Turnrow, Connecticut Review, Stone Canoe,* and W. W. Norton's anthology *Flash Fiction Forward* (2006). He published his first novel, *My Life at First Try,* with Counterpoint Press in 2008.

Of course, a story doesn't have to be short to be good. Some stories never end. A case in point, a Russian folktale about a priest. It goes like this: A priest had a dog. He loved it. The dog ate a piece of meat. The priest killed the dog and wrote on its tombstone that a priest had a dog. That he loved it. That the dog ate a piece of meat. And so on.

This story is a Möbius strip. A snake with its tail in its mouth. I like shorter snakes, though. My definition, 500 words or less. Otherwise, it becomes an anaconda. It's hard to handle an anaconda, and to tame it you need time most people don't have.

Flash fiction is re-incarnated brevity. In our warming world, brevity is green. In our world of competing media, brevity is nimble. In our world where time is the most precious commodity, brevity is eternal.

As a teacher of flash, I tell my students to taste a story. Mouth it. Throw a word or two or a whole sentence away. See if the story still stands. If it does, that word or sentence didn't belong there in the first place. (Standing in front of a marble slab with his chisel, Michelangelo would understand.)

As an editor of a flash fiction magazine, I look for a story that hits me in the face. The protagonist must desire something and her desire has to reach its crescendo by the 500th word. The object of her desire doesn't have to be big, but it's important to her and it's important to the reader.

All writers, even the shy ones, flash themselves; that's what they do either for a living or at least out of a pent-up desire to share. When a reader opens a book, the writer has only a few seconds to grab her with a gripping opening. If he loses that chance, there is no recovery. But even if he succeeds in capturing the reader's attention, then the writer will still have to manage to bring the story to a logical conclusion within the confines of a limited space so that the reader will return again.

After all, a writer is a professional exhibitionist. The reader is the voyeur he hopes to lure.

ᴄᴙ

A FLASH FICTION EXERCISE

Write three flash fiction stories in which each consecutive one is half the length of the previous story in terms of the number of words.

Make sure each story's plot and the set of characters are exactly the same. Note: This exercise was inspired by Bruce Taylor's story "Exercise," which appeared in Issue 7 of *Vestal Review* magazine and is reprinted below.

A STORY EXAMPLE

Exercise

(258 words)

They have said nothing to each other for weeks except what matters to the day, the children, the budget or the dog. He is upstairs at his office window. She is reading in a chaise longue in the shade some book her recently widowed mother gave her. She sighs, he imagines, at how it was an easy mistake for a young girl to make, a less likely error, perhaps, for a man so much older.

Who remembers mostly a white dress, a waist your hands could fit around, the scent of Juicy Fruit and Noxzema. When he asks what's wrong, she always says she's happy; the only thing is, if he were sometimes a little happier a little more often too…

What she thinks of him now he doesn't even know, but fears it's so much less than what she thought at first, when he was what he can't imagine now, and obviously isn't to her now, and why and why? In the grief of his fifties, hard liquor sits him down to pray.

They treat each other as tenderly at least as they'd treat a relative or friend, a needy stranger or the obligatory guest. Whatever it is they might be discussing escapes to the underside of the birch leaves in the gathering breeze. The lights across the river are brighter and seem more distant than the stars. The swallows give way to the bats and a tiny spider spins at the ruined screen a web someone less desperate might be tempted to take as a metaphor.

(130 words)

They have said nothing to each other for weeks except what matters to the day, the children, the budget or the dog. He is upstairs at his office window. She sighs, he imagines, at where love has led her and how it was an easy mistake for a young girl to make.

He remembers a white dress, a waist your hands could fit around, the scent of Juicy Fruit and Noxzema—he wants to ask her what she remembers.

They treat each other as tenderly at least as they'd treat a relative or friend, a needy stranger or the obligatory guest. Whatever it is they might be discussing escapes to the underside of the birch leaves. The lights across the river are brighter and seem more distant than the stars.

(63 words)

They have said nothing to each other for weeks except what matters to the day. She sighs at where love has led her. He remembers a white dress. They treat each other as they'd treat a stranger. Whatever they might be discussing escapes to the underside of the birch leaves. The lights across the river are brighter and more distant than the stars.

—Bruce Taylor, from *Vestal Review*

Pia Z. Ehrhardt

PLASTER DUST AND
SLEEPING JOCKEYS
Tapping Your Story for Load-Bearing Sentences

I live in New Orleans, and my husband and I are in the beginning stages of renovating our hundred-year-old home. Our place used to be a boarding house for jockeys because our neighborhood is close to the Fair Grounds Race Track. (Opened in 1852, it's America's oldest racing site.) On the second floor of our house, shooting off the landing, there are four bed-rooms that don't seem to know about each other, and two bathrooms with fixtures and tiles from the twenties. There are a crazy number of doors. For boarders, it must've been madcap and lively, but for one fam-ily, it's chopped up with no flow, no sightlines, so we're going to integrate the floor plan up there, which means that engineers have been poking around, trekking down to the basement, tapping and worrying as they try to figure out which walls are bearing the weight, which walls can come down. The house can't stand without these load-bearing walls, but they don't exactly call attention to themselves. They aren't thicker or prettier than the other walls. They aren't as obvious as columns.

Load-bearing walls in houses run perpendicular to ceilings made of joists. They hold weight and oppose downward forces, which got me thinking about how flash fictions contain joist-like sentences, but also

Born in Philadelphia, Pennsylvania, *Pia Z. Ehrhardt* now lives in New Orleans, where she substitute teaches at New Orleans Center for Creative Arts and tutors in the charter schools. A contributing editor to *Narrative Magazine* (which awarded her the 2005 Narrative Prize for fiction), her stories, flash fictions, and essays have appeared widely in such journals as *McSweeney's Quarterly, Mississippi Review, Oxford American,* and *Quick Fiction,* and she is anthologized in W. W. Norton's *New Sudden Fiction* (2006). In 2007, her short story collection, *Famous Fathers & Other Stories,* was published by MacAdam/Cage (which is slated to publish her first novel). Frederick Barthelme called *Famous Fathers* "a stunning first collection." Ehrhardt's work has also been featured on NPR's Selected Shorts, and she provided the introduction to the short short collection *A Peculiar Feeling of Restlessness* (2008).

sentences where the energy settles, the focus tightens, and the truths that bear (bare) the story become clear. Sometimes this clarity comes toward the end, sometimes it's in the first paragraph. In my own stories, the load-bearing sentence is usually a line that feels like a mistake, a change in direction—oops! How'd that get in there? The better question is: Why'd that get in there? Often it's a line that embarrasses me, like flashing open your bathrobe and then, too late, covering up again, because once someone sees you naked, you can't take it back. The line presents itself. I wrote it and now it's on the page, holding up the story. What do I want you to know about my characters that shames and frightens—or exhilarates—me? And how did my story go from something I wanted to tell you to something I'm afraid for you to know, but that I must now talk about?

Sometimes these load-bearing walls appear in the early draft, and sometimes in later revisions, but I find that one way to get to them quickly is to put a time constraint on the writing of the story. A few years ago, *McSweeney's* website ran a 20-minute story-writing contest, which turned out to be a Come to Jesus for me because it forced me to sit my butt in the chair, write with purpose, get up to the arc and then down the other side more quickly than I usually would. No snack breaks because the clock was ticking. No pausing for the internal editor to interrupt the flow of the story. All I had time for was the story's business.

The flash fiction you'll find below won an honorable mention in *McSweeney's* Twenty-Minute Stories Contest. Read it, and see if you can find the story's load-bearing sentence that surprised and unsettled me.

I didn't completely understand it, but I respected that it had worked its way into my story. Although this is a piece about a near disaster (that really happened), it's also a piece about the moment you see your father stripped bare by a careless decision, which in turn strips his daughter bare, which opens up this new world of a parent who's no longer infallible. The load-bearing line speaks to a loss of innocence and of privacy, and to an entry into a world of future sex and mistakes, into the solitude of deciding for yourself what's germane and what's inconsequential.

And what about the mother? How did the destroyed car fall on her? Did she also lose her faith in her husband that night?

The story happened, but I left something out. What my mother told me the night I asked her about the car was this: my father had wanted my sister and me to stay in the jump seats and he was going to push and then jump in and make the turn into the garage, but she talked him out of doing this and stayed with him for 30 more years, until he left her and married his graduate student. This recently revealed detail would make the story about something else: blame. The story would then be hers, not mine, a construction in need of its own load-bearing wall.

A FLASH FICTION EXERCISE

Try one. Write a story from start to finish, in 20 uninterrupted minutes. Place your watch where you can see it. Writing under time pressure may force you to give up some bit of truth you didn't know you knew. Find the load-bearing sentence, the place you might be veering around or ignoring, the line you're tempted to delete, and let it bear the story's weight. The line that made me uncomfortable? "It fell obscenely with the bottom up, like a girl on her back with no underwear."

Trust the sentence. Trust why you're there. You may find yourself in an old house of remembered rooms and hiding spots that—no matter how much you poke around—isn't going to fall down on your head.

A STORY EXAMPLE

A Car

My father brought home a turquoise Porsche with red leather upholstery. My sister and I were small, eight and six, and fit tightly in the jumpseats behind my parents.

We went for a ride, tooled around Rome, circled the Colosseum, showing off for the people looking. My father made us listen to him double-clutch because he said that this was good for the car. The sound of this felt like a struggle for the engine, a hesitation, and then the car sped on.

We'd parked along the Via Veneto, the car within eyeshot so my father and mother could admire it at the curb. My sister and I ordered gelati and my parents had coffees spiked with grappa. Everything alcoholic in Italy tasted like licorice.

We lived in an apartment building with a steep driveway, and the car stalled half a block from home. My father made us get out, and he pushed it, one hand on the steering wheel, the other on the open door. When he got to the top of the driveway he thought he would push it and then jump in, coast to the bottom, and park it in the underground garage, but when he pushed the Porsche the car took off. He tried to hang on but it was heavy. The car dragged him and his shoes skidded along the driveway and my mother and sister and I watched in shock. I remember thinking then: You can't hold back a moving car.

The car went down the incline and over a wall and it fell two stories below onto a street that was usually filled with children. It fell obscenely with the bottom up, like a girl on her back with no underwear.

People came running from everywhere, and my father walked down, calmly, to look over the wall. No one was killed, but the car had flattened and my sister and I watched the tow truck pick it up, turn it over, and bring it away. The pretty blue paint had scraped away and the car was smashed up and gray.

My father never spoke about this and my mother didn't either, until they'd divorced and we were on her patio having a glass of wine. She admitted he'd been drinking, but that's all. Not that he had a trip-up on commonsense, shit logic—man, car, incline, fast, crash, death that escaped him that night—and for the next thirty years I was on the lookout for the other things he might do.

—Pia Z. Ehrhardt, from *McSweeney's*

Rusty Barnes

EDITING AND REVISING
FLASH FICTION
How to COAP

Night Train, the journal I co-founded and oversee, has since its inception in 2002 featured flash fiction via competitions and the inclusion of several flash fiction pieces in each issue. Since 2007, when we switched to a primarily online format, we've featured a new piece of flash fiction every week. In the process of choosing and publishing so many stories, and in my own process of revision and writing, with the help of Chris Anderson's wonderful book *Free/Style* (Houghton Mifflin, 1992), I've developed benchmarks for editing the flash fiction we publish. Anderson's book, designed for English composition courses, discusses a process he calls "COAPing with revision" (**C**ut/**O**rder/**A**dd/**P**olish), which is readily adaptable to personal and creative writing.

"C"

Presumably, if you've chosen to publish a story, the quality is beyond question, and what you're looking for when editing and/or revising is a way to push the story beyond the limits of publishable greatness and onto the hallowed grounds of stories-that-must-be-reread. The first step is deciding whether or not the material you have is sufficiently pared down. This is the only guideline for flash fiction in its multifarious forms

Rusty Barnes grew up in rural northern Appalachia, where much of his writing is set. He received a BA from Mansfield University and went on to receive an MFA in Creative Writing from Emerson College. His fiction, poetry, and nonfiction have appeared in journals such as *Barn Owl Review*, *Small Spiral Notebook*, *SmokeLong Quarterly*, *Red Rock Review*, and *Post Road*. After editing fiction for the *Beacon Street Review* (now *Redivider*) and *Zoetrope All-Story Extra*, he co-founded *Night Train*, a literary journal that has been featured in the *Boston Globe*, the *New York Times*, and on National Public Radio. Sunnyoutside Press published a collection of his flash fiction, *Breaking it Down*, in 2007. Find more information at www.rustybarnes.com.

that everyone seems to agree on. A thousand words is a good cut-off, generally. Over the years, I've noticed in other journals that stories between
1,000 and 1,750 words don't seem to be published very often, so *Night
Train* seeks to provide an outlet for those orphaned tweeners by calling
for a slightly longer story, up to 1,500 words. Other journals call for as few
as 500 words. In any case, brevity is clearly the only key.

So what can be cut from a story? This goes further than simply elimi-
nating adjectives and adverbs, the mere paring of words themselves. One
place to begin is with your characters: there is room, generally, for no
more than two or three acting characters in a work of flash fiction. Often,
writers find themselves with a great central character whose progress or
lack thereof is followed through on very well, and an extraneous character or two—color characters, let's say—who can be summarily excised,
and should be, because they don't advance the story. That's a first step. A
second step might be to cut extraneous detail.

Many writers, when faced with a short piece, take the poetic approach,
and fall back on their descriptive abilities as opposed to advancing the
narrative line.[1] This is generally a mistake. Apt detail, to use a boxing metaphor, is the constant jab of writing, and excessive detail like trying for a
knockout with a wild haymaker. Jab throughout, and save the haymaker
for the end, is often my advice. Some people have the energy and brio to
throw haymakers throughout, and more power to them—it all depends
on the story, each case being different. For most of us, though, the time
to let your freak flag fly is in the first draft, and exercising a little restraint
and order is the best approach for editing and revising.

Minimalism, the popularized Carveresque style many stories are
written in these days, nearly *demands* this kind of restraint but bear in
mind you must be careful to edit and revise on the story's own terms; if
a piece's strengths are in its excesses, by all means, encourage the writer
and try not to revise according to your own aesthetic, but instead try to

---

[1]This is one way to tell the difference between a prose poem and a piece of short short
fiction: where the description is amped up at the expense of advancing a story line,
chances are you're looking at a prose poem. Of course, a prose poem can advance a story
line, and a story must rely on description, too. Ain't equivocation grand? The point being,
description for its own sake is a hallmark of poetic technique in and of itself, whereas in a
story the description must serve a purpose other than calling attention to itself as object.

understand what the writer is trying to do and how well she or he accomplishes it. This seems intuitive, but in my experience bears repeating. A fixed aesthetic is the enemy of the editor and reviser. It's all well and good to trumpet your vision of the story over someone else's as a point of discussion, but in practice, you run the risk of pissing off writers, and worse, making their stories conform. Your job as editor is to make the piece the best it can be on its own terms. Careful word-to-word attention is really the only qualification an editor needs, other than to have read nearly everything, to have considered its aesthetic value, and to be beholden to none of it.

"O"

After you've cut everything you possibly can, it's time to put what pieces you have in their best order. This is probably the most difficult element of editing and revising. Every story's organic form is set in every writer's mind and woe to the editor who makes a suggestion. It either goes really well, or horribly wrong. I generally suggest these types of changes only when I have a previous relationship with the writer or otherwise have reason to believe they can take the suggestion in the spirit it's intended. There are questions you can ask yourself as you edit and revise, however, that make the process easier:

- If the story is one that depends on linear narrative, how well is the line delineated? Often, writers will try to deepen their narratives by adding subplots where they might be better served by concentrating on the main thread of the story. When in doubt, refer to step one: *cut*.

- If the story is not linear, how does it move the reader forward? Is it consistent in the demands it makes on a reader? If the story meanders, what do you take the purpose of the meandering to be, and will it be clear enough to a reader without further signposting? It's tricky to edit a nonlinear story simply because we've often been taught—by many narratives, television and film plots, and creative writing instructors—to want a straight line where the jump-cut and wobble make more sense (again keeping the story's and writer's aims in mind), but it can be done, only with the strictest of attention. Not a half-assed process, in other words, but a careful commitment to treat the writer's attempt seriously and to help them find the means by which the story can be told most effectively.

- If the story is a found/form piece[2] (i.e., dependent on using the matrices of a nonnarrative), which is increasingly common these days, how does that form subvert the narrative in satisfying ways, and what can you do to enhance its effect?

"A"

Adding material might be the most overrated means of deepening a story. It's necessary, yes, but as a proponent of flash fiction for years now, the sheer number of bloated 5–8,000-word stories I read saddens me. Call it the shrinking American attention span or whatever you'd like; the fact is that stories are getting shorter by the moment.

There might be many reasons for this, but something I've thought about for years, prompted by a long-ago essay by Sven Birkerts, is the sheer amount of information we're hammered with on a daily basis. Aside from the myth of multitasking—already proven to decrease attention and productivity—there's the incredible amount of three-act or otherwise linear narrative we've been force-fed over the years via the media and many books as well. The short story medium is crying out for a new approach, and the necessary shortening of narrative make sense. We've absorbed so many tropes, we often recognize them near-immediately and can fill in so many of the typical details that "normal" slow revelation makes little sense, and we have little patience for it. Somewhere between the linear narrative and the post-postmodern fracturing of narrative there might be a third way, dependent on its brevity as its primary descriptor. Interlinked short to very-short narratives might be the beginning of that third way, or of *another way*, at least. The main antecedent is clearly Hemingway, and practiced *in extremis* by contemporary writ-

---

[2] A kind of story that uses, for example, traffic signs as narrative signposts, or a modified self-help book form, or an interview form—or in one example from *Night Train*—the form of an alumni bulletin, to achieve its fictional aims. If there's an appropriate term for this, let me know.

ers like Diane Williams and Richard Currey, Larry Fondation and Kim Chinquee (p. 109), whose work often consists of minimal paragraphs that suggest the forward motion of a larger narrative without actually becoming linear in the sense we normally think of narrative, and where adding more text would slacken their incredible tightness.

When it's necessary to add, though, it's nearly always only what might have been excised in the first step of the editing/revising process. The idea being that once the fat is pared away completely, you can better see where the grain of the meat is, and can add back those elements of the narrative that best serve the writer's overall purpose. Often, it's a matter of one explanatory clause or a particularly apt metaphor that makes a piece leap beyond itself into another realm of expertise or impact, a realm in which it's only necessary to polish and perfect what's already there.

"P"

Polishing is where an editor comes in most handy. There's the copyedit process in which infelicitous phrases are dealt with and matters of house style reestablished, of course, but more important, here is where the editor can suggest subtleties in rhythm and variances in punctuation. I find myself adding paired em-dashes most often, with the semicolon close behind,[3] and god forgive the inappropriate splicer of commas. I love a well-placed splice, but the writer who insists on them as some measure of respect for stream-of-consciousness writing had best go elsewhere looking for publication; it's not likely to fly with me unless it's effing brilliant, in which case all bets are out the window, I'm happy to say.

Cutting, ordering, adding, polishing. It's a simple four-step editing/revising method that works for any kind of writing, but is particularly suited to flash fiction because its first step demands the kind of attention that should be paid to any kind of prose sent out for publication. It's particularly important for this short-form story, which defies all description *except* by its brevity. This brevity provides a framework for thinking about

---

Why don't writers use the semicolon more often? This mystifies me. It's my favorite punctuation mark by far.

the writing as mere wordage in service to the larger idea of the story, its individual aesthetics, and the writer's, too. Words become a means to an end—as in a linear story—when the narrative demands it; and words become the focus themselves—as in a nonlinear story—when it does not.

A FLASH FICTION EXERCISE
Memory-Mapping

I acknowledge here the conflation/adaptation of a couple of exercises from Josip Novakovich's essential book *Fiction Writer's Workshop* (Story Press, 1995), the "Settings" chapter in particular. Where Novakovich asks writers to use lists of objects remembered from the childhood home and descriptions of the childhood neighborhood to imagine what happened in those places, using a map if necessary, I take the exercise in a different, character-generating direction. I've used this generative exercise successfully to jump-start students having difficulty finding material they're sufficiently invested in, as well as for beginners who have trouble moving away from the autobiographical in their work.

First, imagine your childhood home in as great a detail as you can. Take a room, at first, and imagine every object in it. Draw a map; it needn't be artful at all. If that proves insufficient, widen the scope; imagine the entire house, or the entire area around your childhood home. This should take 15 minutes or so. Now, and this is key, imagine all the members of your family interacting in that space. What happened there? Or more important, what might happen there? What might be the precipitating *event*?

Families are full of conflict, as we all know, and to take the autobiographical question out of the equation—I trust most families don't want their business told in fiction—imagine each individual with their exact opposite characteristics. Mix it up, and have fun. If Uncle Vinny was a kraut-eating truck driver with bad football knees and a sycophantic streak toward the Steelers, make him Uncle Denny who graduated from Harvard Law and has three noisy children, two boys and a girl, who constantly play farting games at the family reunion.

Once all that fun stuff is done; write. See what happens.

This exercise, especially if you set yourself a word limit, can often result in stories incredibly rich in detail, and rife with intense emotions. *Night Train,* in 2007, published a story by Lydia Copeland, which contains the richness and emotion this exercise can bring out with the proper attention paid.

A STORY EXAMPLE

In the Air a Shining Heart

In the air a shining heart, wet lungs releasing and releasing, your sweet milk head, your pulsating skin. Only an inch separates us. A shimmer of hot air trembles like boiling water above the highway. There are seeds floating in the sky. These things will become other things. A plume of purple. An orange wing. A hazel eye. A grain of rice. In the air, a curl of baby hair, a pale face and flushed cheeks, a shred of coconut in the palm of my hand. We both wonder where I'm going. I've been to the ocean and felt my body sink away. I've stood against the skyline with the other honeymooners and let the man I love kiss each button of my shirt, down to the very x of thread. I've felt his hand beneath the hem of my skirt warm as a tongue. I've lived alone in old and dark houses. Now I drive. Now I stop in towns that are still wet behind the ears. I eat their lunches and sleep in their beds. I swallow their water. I find their high schools and walk the track fields at night. The stadium lights shine above bleachers lighting the new grasses and chain-link fences. The mornings all mingle together. The same pillowcases, the same cups of coffee, the same cool engine, the same drip of oil. In the air, the pitch of a muted television, sheets that smell like baking bread. A boy named Ezra. A boy named Gwyn. I try these things on for you to see how they fit, to see who is loose around the edges and who is like a glove. Who comes home for dinner and who plays in traffic? The corn is tossing in the field along the road. Beneath the green and white silk, silver beads gleam like rows of teeth, like the pearls that will one day swell from your mouth. There will be a jar of light by your bed, curtains that let the seasons into the room, a closet big enough to hide inside. You will rub your cheek against the tip of your shirt collar. You will wipe dirty hands into the carpet. You will sleep off sickness in this room. In the air a heat grows and water drips from lips. I drive until I hear "Nights in White Satin" twice on the radio. The different stations fade into static then appear again clean and new. There are fields and orchards on either side of me. The farmers here watch for deer in their crops. The deer always come in groups, a doe and two fawns or several does and no fawns. They come soft in the night through blanketed woods to eat winter squash and green beans from the vine. The farmers here listen for foxes. They have memorized the sound of an arched back. They know red and they know silver. They install bat houses and little irrigation systems made from upside-down soda liters. Their tomatoes are perfect red globes. Their cucumbers swell with wet flesh and flat white seeds. When I drive I don't think about these things. I don't see the golden apples or the pea pods. Instead I taste them at the end of the day when I'm resting on a bed in an overly cool room. My eyes are closed and then there is the shape of grapes and warm patches of light. In the air, all the pills lined up on the edge of my mother's sink, a soft white hand with pretty pink nails. A spare key, a blank expression, the smell of a hot iron. There are two notes, one old and one new. The new note is like poetry. The old note is straight to the point. I remember thin wrists and dangling bracelets, all the dresses laid out on the bedspread, the shoes that matched even though no one would see them. In the air, alligators hide in the marsh, their eyes never blinking. Dust coats the skin. Plants grow under water, under fake oceans and wash up limp and soggy in some dark place on a fake beach. My skin stretches until I can see the bottom. You grow tight like a muscle. The pressure of your body trips me up, makes me think I can't walk a straight line. Only a few moments separate us. In the air, nameless things or forgotten names. Soon it will be ten years since the words were written out and the door was broken down. No one knows what makes the body shudder. We think cold, we think pain. We think the blackness that spreads inside when someone leaves. I was alone then in a room with two beds and a window. I used to watch the heli-pad lights on the hospital roof. They flashed green, then white, then orange. The tricolors of some country's flag. In those days that followed, I didn't wear a seatbelt. I didn't look for oncoming traffic. I didn't eat. I was mostly bones. And black sank like a rock into the pit of me, always in the back seats of cars watching the naked trees reel by, listening to someone else's favorite song. In the end, the relatives will cheer. They will remark on your opened eyes and how you seem to take everything in and check it off a secret list. *Things Never Seen by This Here Boy*. One night we will wait for your fever to break. We'll place wet cloths on your forehead. We'll brush the drops of sweat from your nose. One day you will cry and cry until the sound coming out of you is only a soft whimper that no one can hear. One day you will ask me if animals can live inside of us. You will see a blue eye like a cat's look-ing back at you when you rub your eyelids at night. You will wonder what is real and what is imagined. You will wonder if animals watch you when you sleep, if they follow you into dreams. I will tell you only what I remember, that there are habits impossible to break and that sometimes the essence of you doesn't like to use the telephone or put the dishes away, and the only things that live inside us are histories that rise and sink and shift in bed with you at night. They wait like promises in towns not yet visited, in your taste, in the pages of a book. Eventually, you will forget that the milk is more water than cream. You will remember it as a sweet cordial in your mouth, but one day something will remind you. It will be a mood in the air, a slow evaporation lifting like a veil. It will be cold sun on a sidewalk, a cloud of breath. People in their houses will look out and look into you. You will walk with your arms crossed over your chest and a black dog following behind you. You with your books and new sneakers. You with your round face and chocolate eyes singing and singing.

—Lydia Copeland, from *Night Train*

Bruce Holland Rogers

WRITING FIXED-FORM NARRATIVES
Who's Going to Stop You?

Unlike your generic bird guide, such as *The Birds of Central America*, a field guide for flash fiction cannot be absolutely complete because, while there are only so many Central American birds, the species count for flash fiction can't be enumerated. A complete guide would have to anticipate species that haven't yet appeared. That's why I'm dissatisfied with most definitions of flash fiction.

Definitions by length are for editorial convenience. For the editors of *Collier's* (an American magazine published from 1888 to 1955), a short short was a story that fit on one page of their magazine. The editors of the original *Flash Fiction* anthology—James Thomas, Denise Thomas, and Tom Hazuka—picked 750 words as an upper limit because this could be printed on two facing pages of a digest-size literary magazine. Page layout and word-count definitions don't say much about the experience of reading or writing short shorts, however.

I do like the definition offered by fellow writer Kate Wilhelm in her introduction to my short short collection *Flaming Arrows*. As Kate expresses it, a novel invites the reader to explore an entire house, down to snooping in the closets; a short story requires that the reader stand

Bruce Holland Rogers is internationally known for his science fiction writing and his experimentation with the short prose form. Born in Tucson, Arizona, he has lived in many places, but he recently returned to Oregon. Rogers has lectured and spoken frequently (on creative writing in general and the fixed form in particular) at universities in London, Lisbon, and Vienna, and at writers conferences and literary festivals. His award-winning flash fiction has been translated into two-dozen languages and is available by email subscription through www.shortshortshort.com. Rogers is the author of four flash fiction story collections, the most recent of which won the World Fantasy Award (*The Keyhole Opera*, 2005). He teaches fiction writing for the Whidbey Writers Workshop MFA, a program of the Northwest Institute of Literary Arts.

outside of an open window to observe what's going on in a single room; and a short short requires the reader to kneel outside of a locked room and peer in through the keyhole. For me, that captures an essential characteristic of most short shorts. They are not just short, but also, typically, compressed.

Wilhelm's metaphor is evocative and apt, but as a definition, still incomplete. It does not distinguish between flash fiction and its close cousins. In the Short Forms course I teach, which covers flash fiction, prose poems, and brief narrative prose, the MFA students and I frequently debate whether a particular piece published as a poem is really a story, or vice versa. Some pieces that I wrote as flash fiction have been published as poems or nonfiction. Even if we can agree about which pieces are narrative prose poems and which are very short stories, not every piece of flash fiction is compressed. Some are short simply because their scope is narrow. And, again, writers are inventing new genre-defying tricks all the time.

Since definitions are hard to pin on a moving target, I don't sweat definitions much. For me flash fiction is short. It's narrative. It's what I write. I enjoy the debates about classification, but mostly as an excuse to have other debaters bring me interesting stories to consider.

Most fundamentally for me, the essence of flash fiction is in how I experience it as a reader and working writer. Flash fiction is fleeting and ephemeral. I will even venture as far as to say that in career terms, anyway, flash fiction is lightweight stuff.

Them's fighting words, to be sure. They may seem odd coming from a writer who specializes in the form. Flash fiction is my passion and the source of most of my writing income. What's more, some short short stories stick in my memory as sacred texts. They continue to resonate years after I first read them. Indeed, those are just the sorts of stories that I hope I'm writing at least some of the time, stories that, for all their brevity, strike a deep and life-enhancing chord.

However, short short stories do melt fast. And that can be a good thing.

Because flash fiction is so short, the experience of reading it will never be as immersive as reading a novel. As I begin reading a short short, I am already aware of the approach of the final line. If I don't like this particular story, the brevity is reassuring. I'm only a few lines from the next story, which I may like better. As a result, I don't mind if the writer takes risks and even tries my patience with a strange technique or with subject matter I would dismiss if it required more of my time. Thanks to brevity, I'll try anything. I may even enjoy strange storytelling techniques that would grate in a longer story.

Flash fiction is professionally ephemeral, too. Any single short short story does little to establish a writer's reputation. For good or for ill, a short short, or even a whole collection of flash fiction, does far less to make a professional mark than a novel does. But this means that the writer of short shorts is free to write whatever he or she wants to write.

I'm a writer who enjoys being all over the genre map. I write science (SF), literary, mystery, western, and fantasy fiction, plus fables and fairy tales. As a novelist, I could never operate this way, at least not under a single byline. Market pressures dictate that a novelist must give readers and publishers a similar experience from one book to the next. Because flash fiction is so unimportant in establishing a reputation, I can *play*.

Yes, I do think that, story by story, a writer of flash fiction can build an audience and a reputation, just as a poet does. I'm certainly not saying that because flash fiction is ephemeral, it doesn't have to be good, no more that I would say that about poetry. I want every story I write to be a good story. But if I write some oddball short short stories using oddball methods . . . who is going to object?

So I do play. I grow stories out of unpromising material. I draft stories based on some trick of technique, such as writing the narrative only in questions or in denials. I look at nonliterary writing—warning labels or lists of ingredients, say—and try to invent stories using a similar format, vocabulary, or tone. But one of my favorite modes of play is writing fiction to fixed forms, and that's an approach that I invite other flash fiction writers to attempt.

Fixed forms are common in poetry. Such forms have rules. An English sonnet will be 14 lines long. Each line will be about 10 syllables of iambic pentameter. The first line will rhyme with the third; the second, with the fourth. Lines 13 and 14 will rhyme with each other and will, together, mark a change in the poem by summing up all that went before or by providing a sudden contrast or a new perspective. And so on. Any of the technical aspects of a poem can be prescribed in advance to define a fixed form.

In the same way, fiction writers can prescribe characteristics for a short short story before writing the story, either by inventing a fixed form or adapting one from poetry. How many sentences? How many words in each sentence? Must some word or idea repeat at intervals? Is there a point-of-view switch that has to occur at a particular point? A prose sonnet might consist of 14 sentences instead of 14 lines. Instead of end-rhyming, it might use internal rhymes. A prose villanelle could consist of 19 paragraphs instead of 19 lines and repeat phrases or themes in the same pattern that the poem employs.

One of the simplest constraints to work with is a set word count. The now-defunct magazine *NFG* used to feature stories of exactly 69 words (not including the title). Here's one of mine:

What Are You Using for Bait?

He comes into the Manitowish bait shop every day, asking beginner's questions and lingering at her counter. Friday he holds a fish he says he's caught. She thinks, A salmon? In Wisconsin? She doesn't let on. He's going to grill it. Does she want to come? Her last boyfriend was a liar, too. But she likes salmon. She figures she can take the bait and spit out the hook.

The challenge of telling a story in so few words shapes which ideas you can develop, but for a 69-word story, I generally have to have an idea of where I'm going before I start writing. With an even more constraining form, one that determines the exact word count for each sentence, I can start writing before I know where I'm going. For example, I devised a "Fibonacci sonnet"[1] form consisting of two paragraphs. The word counts of sentences and the relative proportions of the paragraphs are deter-

---

[1] Leonardo Fibonacci, a thirteenth-century mathematician, is associated with the "Fibonacci numbers," a sequence that he did not discover, but wrote about. The sequence is created by adding the last two numbers in the sequence to get the next number: 0, 1, 1, 2, 3, 5, 8, 13, 21, and so on. The higher the numbers, the more closely the ratio between two adjacent numbers approximates the golden ratio, a proportion that is often found in nature and that artists since the Renaissance have believed to be aesthetically pleasing.

mined by the sequence of Fibonacci numbers. In the first paragraph, the sentences are of a set length in words: 1, 1, 2, 3, 5, 8, 13, 21, 34, and 55. In the second paragraph, the first sentence is again 34^2 words long and counts the same series back down: 21, 13, 8, 5, 3, 2, 1, 1.

Renaissance

Snow. Ice. Heavy skies. All flights delayed. Morris wished he could smoke. He wished that he could go stand outside. This is what life becomes, he thought, watching ice collect on grounded wings. The career he'd expected to take him to London and Paris brought him repeatedly to Omaha or this airport in Billings. It wasn't that he was dissatisfied, exactly, with his wife or the way that his kids had turned out, or with the split-level in Cherry Creek and the condo in Vail they hardly used. But a blizzard like this made everything smaller, as if the world had contracted around this terminal and Morris and his fellow passengers were the last people at the end of time, stuck here to consider what their lives had amounted to so far, forced in the light of that awareness to begin new lives.

In his new life, Morris would marry the girl sitting across from him chewing gum and reading a fashion magazine, dangling one shoe from her toes, although they would have nothing to talk about. In his new life, he would not care what anyone thought, what the safe investments were, or whether smoking was allowed. And under the circumstances, why shouldn't he smoke, for the love of Pete? Why shouldn't he take a stand right now? He felt inside his pocket. Where's the lighter? Some lint. Coins. *There*.

Opening with sentence fragments of one or two words generally means that for the first 3 sentences (sentence fragments, really), my task is limited to finding 4 suitable words. In selecting words, I begin to narrow my setting or subject matter, but only as the sentences become longer do I

---

[2] A Petrarchan or Italian sonnet has an octave of eight lines followed by a sestet of six, and this ratio of 8:6 (1.33333) is very roughly similar to the golden ratio of approximately 1.618033. The Fibonacci sonnet intends to come much closer to the golden ratio. There are 144 words in the first paragraph and 89 in the second, for a ratio of about 1.617977. Of course, there is no real point to this fussy attempt to get close to the golden ratio, any more than the rules of a verse sonnet specify fourteen lines and not fifteen or thirteen.

begin to discover more of my story. The fixed form allows me to discover my story as I write it.

Some writers will see this description of fixed-form writing and immediately be drawn to such experiments because they sound fun. For others, fixed-form narrative will sound absurd. The former group will need no coaxing in order to try fixed forms. To the latter, let me suggest that this approach to writing is something to save for a day when you want to write, but can't come up with an appealing idea. A Fibonacci sonnet or a word loop (see exercise below) is the kind of project you can undertake when you don't feel clever enough to generate a story. In writing such a piece, your focus doesn't have to be on a story. All you have to be able to generate is sentences to, as it were, fill in the form. Drafting a fixed-form story may lead you to an idea that you express more conventionally in the next draft. That is, you can throw away the form and keep working on the story.

Ultimately, the ideal is for the form to go unnoticed, or almost unnoticed. A story has to work as a story, and "following the rules" of a fixed form is no excuse for a story that feels awkward or incomplete. Fixed forms, whether they are just a way of getting the story started or are your objective for the final draft, become merely the medium. What matters, as always, is the effect of your story on the reader.

So here's to your own exploration of fixed forms of prose. I hope you'll enjoy playing with the fixed forms that other writers have already invented and, if so inclined, will even experiment with inventing fixed forms of your own. Perhaps you'll create a fixed form that other writers will want to use. In terms of a field guide, that's like discovering an entirely new species.

A FLASH FICTION EXERCISE

Write a word loop (see my example below). The first word of your story will also be the last word. The last word of each sentence must be the first word of the following sentence. Where you can, for the sake of surprise and variety, try to use the repeating word in a different sense, such as *fall*, the name of the season, and *fall*, the verb.

Concentrate your efforts on the sentence in front of you, and don't worry too much about how you're going to make your way to the final word. You'll get there. A word loop requires a balance between steering and allowing yourself to drift.

A STORY EXAMPLE

The House of Women

Women were all I knew of family. Family meant a household with my mother and three sisters so much older that they loved me without rivalry. Rivalry they reserved for each other. Other boys had fathers who took them hunting. Hunting was, for me, a mystery of guns and blood. Blood mysteries in our house were different.

Different boys came courting my sisters, giving me quarters to go away. Away is where they took my sisters, eventually. Eventually, it was just the two of us, me and my mother in a house I tried to fill with a loud guitar and an old Mustang that spent most of its time on the garage floor in parts. Parts were the vehicle of my initiation, for when my friends were with me we could speak the code of cams and carburetors and go to a country that we imagined was for men alone.

Alone and on my own at last, I found further paths into the world of men. Men working with me at the garage went for beers after work, bowled weekends, hunted in October, all to be away from their wives. Wives and children, they joked, were God's punishment for youth. Youth, they urged me, was meant for raising hell.

Hell-raising, according to my workmates, was a matter of drinking hard and of spending Saturday nights with girls whose names a man would forget by the time he told the story Monday. Monday mornings didn't find me bragging of such exploits, though. Though I went for beers and bowled sometimes and even learned to hunt, I disappointed my adopted brothers. Brothers shouldn't speak with their brothers' wives with quite the ease that I did. Did they think that noticing a different hair style or knowing where to find the shoes to match that handbag was flirting? Flirting was what they called it to my face, though behind my back, they muttered other things. Things at work have improved only slightly since I met and married Bonnie.

Bonnie hoped our first would be a boy, so I haven't shared with her my relief that we're having a girl. Girl one, I hope, of two or three to come. Come to me, my daughters, and bring me home to the house of women.

—Bruce Holland Rogers, from *The Writer*

Julio Ortega

A FLASH BEFORE THE BANG

I. Three working flash definitions

1. When the novel woke up, the flash fiction was already there.

2. "John went out on a trip."

3. The novel can win by points, the short story has to win by KO.

1. The most famous flash fiction in Spanish is by Augusto Monterroso, a devilish Guatemalan who lived as an exile in Mexico. It reads: "When the man woke up, the dinosaur was still there" (*Cuando el hombre despertó, el dinosaurio todavía estaba allí*). A number of readings unfold: a man wakes up and finds himself many centuries ago; dinosaurs are still around, only in another time zone; a man wakes up inside another dream and has to kill the monster to be free. . . . But, also, a series of parallel flash stories are possible: when the man slept, the dinosaur stepped out of the museum; when the dinosaur woke up, men were already extinguished; the man awoke and in the mirror he found a dinosaur.

2. The first story ever, I read somewhere, appears on an ancient Egyptian tablet and declares that "John went out on a trip." How do we know that

A native of Peru, *Julio Ortega* has taught Latin American Literature at Brown University for 20 years. Internationally acclaimed as a critic of such authors as Carlos Fuentes and Gabriel García Márquez, Ortega's own experimental poetry, fiction, and drama has won awards from Lima, Madrid, Paris, and Mallorca. The author of many books and the editor of a number of anthologies, his stories and poems have appeared in *Antaeus, Agni, Yale Lit, London Magazine,* and *Sulfur,* among others. His well-known flash story *"Las Papas"* was reprinted in *Sudden Fiction International* (1989), and recently translated into Farsi. It also appears in his latest book in English translation from Wings Press, *The Art of Reading: Stories and Poems* (2007). "As always," writes Carlos Fuentes, "Ortega's art is insightful."

this is a flash fiction and not a document? Because no one during that time period could have left his town on his own will. Moreover, it encapsulates the high rhetoric of sudden fiction: it has a character (I call him "John," but he has 1,000 names); there is a dominant action (the storytelling is fully present); and what is shown or said happens in time. Not less important, it announces the very rule of any story—the breaking of a code. John is an adventurer who stands against authority and decides to leave, to explore, to know.

3. Julio Cortázar wrote this recommendation to the writer of short stories: you need to score a KO of the reader. Flash fiction can only be resolved by sudden revelation, as wonder. Flash fiction is a fictional truth—an epiphany.

II. A unit of time

I see flash fiction as an allegory of our own fugacity. It is the form of being here, as transients. This is the genre of transhumant reading—it takes place in a transitional language, as substitution and translation.

It is said that we consume time at such velocity that we are probably 20 years ahead of ourselves. The North Pole already melted, our computers are antiques, and bookstores are museums of the book. . . . But short fiction is a time seed, it repudiates the waste of language in a redundant future. Flash fiction stands as an economy of speech; in fact, as saving, drafting, preserving language against the production of residua. We read flash fiction with a feeling of complicity, in a humorous conspiracy. In a few lines, our time circulates freely, within a larger present.

III. An oral tradition

Once, I asked Toni Morrison if black folks flying back to Africa in her books come from Gabriel García Márquez's *One Hundred Years of Solitude.* "No," she answered, "they come from Ohio." It was an oral tradition—she added—that one could find in the countryside, but it disappeared as you approached the cities. But I believe that for both writers, the source is the same: African folklore. In both cases, the story is a form of social control—to leave the violence of society, even to leave their novels, people as well as characters need to flash-fly beyond memory and explanations. Magic realism starts in popular oral sagas, becomes powerful in novels in which imagination is the inner form of truth, and eventually evolves around sudden, memorable epiphanies.

IV. A taxi in Mexico

Currently, I am writing flash fiction not as a flash fiction genre but as a sort of free notation, crossing borders and all genres, in a series that I call *Diario imaginario*, a title that includes *dìa*, which includes *di* ("day" and "say"), as well as *imagen* and the anagram *originario* (*imagen* and *origen*). This hybrid quality of notation is a sort of nomadic condition of language. It moves across the short story, the prose poem, the aphorism, but also the parody, the notation of dreams, and free variations. I use those agendas that include an optimistic blank page for each day of the year. When I write, it is impossible for me to use one imperious fountain pen; I prefer the cheap hotel pens because of the feeling of provisional, momentary writing.

Some years ago in Mexico City, leaving a taxi in downtown, I realized that I was forgetting my notebook—it was a black, thick, British agenda, and I had written a number of pages with all sorts of prose, notes, readings, and thoughts. The yellow cab was starting to leave, and I had the natural impulse to run after it. I could have caught up to that taxi and grabbed my notebook, but I hesitated. Should I let it go? I felt a sudden relief. Not to have to transcribe all those pages, little stories, dreams, and poems . . . ! I watched the taxi leave for good. But I didn't have a sense of loss; I had the feeling of a tribute.

I knew I was going to write a note on the experience ("When the man left his taxi, the book he was writing forgot to go with him"), but I still was afraid (hopeful?) that the taxi driver would find my address and send me the notebook ("The writer wakes up, and his writing was already waiting").

Thus, I found out that every writer (and, for that matter, every person) has a number of unwritten novels in the form of flash fictions. Stories, anecdotes, fragments, that in order to be flash fiction would need to be transcribed within the shape of a fictional piece of writing—or maybe not, perhaps it is up to you to move beyond conventions and to take advantage of another exploration of fact and fiction.

IV. A flash fiction by Juan Rulfo

The Mexican writer Juan Rulfo is the author of two works of fiction, *El llano en llamas* (short stories) and *Pedro Páramo* (a very short novel). Published in 1955, this novel is probably the first masterpiece of the new Latin American narrative, and a decisive influence on both Carlos Fuentes and Gabriel García Márquez. In Puerto Rico, probably in 1983, during a pause in a writers conference, I ended up sitting with Rulfo, and he told me this story about his travels among the peasant towns of his country:

> "It was already late in the night when I arrived at that little, lost town in the mountains. To my surprise, the peasants were waiting for me. In silence, without any explanation, they took me to the plaza. They tied me up to the tree at the center of that plaza, and again in silence, they left. At dawn, they come back, looked at me, and decided to untie me. Finally, one of them spoke. He said: 'We saw you coming from far away. But we realized that you were coming without your soul. Your soul was looking for you. That's why we had to tie you up. Now your soul has found you.'"

Flash fiction wanders, I realize now, between waking up and waking down. The fictional, sudden vision occurs when your own soul finally reaches you and brings a fistful of words.

⁓

A FLASH FICTION PROMPT

Each of the following lines wants to light the spark of fiction. You may continue the series with new propositions, or develop from any of these ten lines your own flash fiction. The challenge is to do more with less. On clearing ashes, and learning from mourning, language can open new associations and provide some resolution.

A STORY EXAMPLE

Ground zero

1. And then, we started by learning another language.

2. In the lack of international news we found our own absence—the need to be part of a larger conversation.

3. Walking around the tables of "new releases," we still wait for a translation from an unknown language.

4. Look in the new listings for the number of foreign films that are not offered.

5. And because television is a local archaism, we were unable to edit a larger view.

6. Migration Day! Let's welcome the new immigrants in a parade dedicated to our future, their memory.

7. Never again should be closed another bridge open for you among the ashes.

8. To this we belong, to a nomadic, nameless tribe, and there we choose a forthcoming citizen-ship.

9. If each perpetuator is equivalent, every victim is unique because violence is inadmissible.

10. And then the value of anyone is in your eyes: alive inside. To see you, beyond the ashes.

—Julio Ortega

Ron Carlson

ON WRITING FLASH FICTION

After a flash an image burns on the eye, the visual echo of the moment.

Don't wait to be ready. Start before you know what you're saying. Hell, start right now.

No, now.

Now.

Put some stuff in the first sentence and carve in a working verb that is slightly out of place and ask it to do something it hasn't done before or been paid to do. It shouldn't exactly fit. By the time you finish it will fit perfectly, own the place, be boss. By stuff, I mean something that we can stand on and sit down in, so the rest can happen. By this explanation, I mean, move from word to deed. It can't just be words. I don't want to give the impression it can just be words. We want more than swirling ectoplasm—unless it is hovering over the neighborhood and some kid just noticed it and pointed. That is, we want more than a posture. So how clever are you? Is the answer ten on the Universal Eight-Bar Clever Scale? We don't care. No matter how short your work, you are responsible for it. You can change your name and you're still responsible. Even if you move, and you'll move. This should give you pause, but not for long.

Ron Carlson grew up in Salt Lake City, Utah. He currently teaches at the University of California–Irvine, after serving many years as director of the creative writing program at Arizona State University. As a teacher he is highly respected for his insight into writing as process and craft. His most recent novel includes *Five Skies* (2007), and his selected stories are in *A Kind of Flying* (2003), most of which appeared on the "Best of" lists of the *New York* and *Los Angeles Times*. In 2007, he published *Ron Carlson Writes a Story*, a small book on the creation of one story. In 2009, his new novel, *Signal,* is slated to be published by Viking. Heavily anthologized and considered a master of the short story, he has published many short shorts.

The moon gave the wolfman paws but not for long. See: avoid puns. He also received claws—they were longer and more convincing. It is important to note that he did not welcome their arrival. He would look at his hands, remember, and they'd start to change, and then he'd look at the night sky. **Key to all fiction, long or short, is to remember that the wolfman did not want the moon.** Everybody else seems to want it and it's all over the place in stories, absolutely stopped in orbit, hanging over every scene after dark. Bring on the moon, moonlight, moonglow, moon over name-your-city, but the wolfman was just a man without it, and fine without it, dreaded it, and even the curtains couldn't help him. How horrible the moon.

It's okay to rhyme. It is not okay to use *wreak havoc* or *warm and cozy*. *Havoc*, of course, alone is fine, and *wreak* is beautiful, but be careful.

I'd say put someone in mortal danger, someone we've never seen before in all the eons of stories, your person, and fresh danger too please, not just drunk driving or a bully or the creeping green toxin, unless it's that green that glows so you can see it coming. No water. No bathtub, like that, or the lake or down by the lake especially at night.

You can have the night if you start writing right now. No, now. Because night is about used up.

Don't use dirty words, such as they are, hoping to jump-start the engine with explosives. It doesn't work. Boom goes the dirty word and then what. Smoke? Not even. Use cozy words that we haven't seen around for a while, some old word with dandruff on its shoulders and ink stain on its shirt pocket.

Key is to stop before you mess up page two. Put something on page one. Don't be cute, even if you majored in it in college. Don't be ironic. That's impossible, but make an effort.

Put the thousand extras with bows and arrows outside the castle. Show the old stone walls of the old fortress quiet in the dawn. You can still use dawn. Be careful with daybreak, dawn's early light and the crack of dawn. I'm serious in all of this. Show inside the fortress, the citizens there listening and afraid. There is an ineffable noise from the field. You can't have three hundred archers waiting in the open and not have some noise: the breathing, the knees creaking, and the whispering of archers.

And now there are small fires and a small fire makes a noise too, the eating of sticks by flame, and this is going to be one of those awesome flaming arrow assaults on the walled city.

I'd like to shoot a flaming arrow. I mean just to see it. I don't have any enemies I would approach with such a thing. I've got enemies, I suppose, both in the fortress and in the open field. I'm sorry to have enemies. I feel misunderstood in that, and I suppose that's why I write, perhaps, the lost love, the torn words broken in the lane. Regardless, some night with the new night cloaking the damp earth, I would really love to hold my arrow over an open fire until the flammable wick blooms yellow, and then I would be careful handling it, notching it in the bow and drawing it back. I'm not an archer, and I don't really want to take up archery, except to shoot the one flaming arrow up into the black sky once. It's never going to happen. Just like the battle I described. Never going to happen. There will always be armies in the fields at night and fear on someone's face and the unalterable sadness of having enemies near and far.

When in doubt, which is where you'll be living your life as a writer of all your work, short or long, write something simple and follow it out past knowing where it flows into the seductive havoc that always waits at the center of our endeavors. You'll be like the ingénue in the basement of the castle with nothing but your nightgown and a candle. Listen. All you can hear is a kind of wet growling. It doesn't sound like your friend Dave, but you'll still call out "Dave?" and move further into the dark with the candle fluttering and the growling growing louder. "Dave?" Even though it doesn't sound like Dave, you've got to proceed barefoot on the cold stone floor. "Dave? Dave?" Don't look at the candle for when it flickers and goes out, your eyes will only see that ghost and not the real dark before you.

Then, however, stay alert. Don't mess up page two.

FURTHER READING

The contributors, editor, and press recommend the following:

ANTHOLOGIES

Brevity & Echo: An Anthology of Short Short Stories. Eds. Abigail Beckel and Kathleen Rooney. Boston: Rose Metal, 2006.

Flash Fiction: 72 Very Short Stories. Eds. James Thomas, Denise Thomas, and Tom Hazuka. New York: Norton, 1992.

Flash Fiction Forward: 80 Very Short Stories. Eds. James Thomas and Robert Shapard. New York: Norton, 2006.

Micro Fiction: An Anthology of Really *Short Stories.* Ed. Jerome Stern. New York: Norton, 1996.

New Sudden Fiction: Short-Short Stories from America and Beyond. Eds. Robert Shapard and James Thomas. New York: Norton, 2007.

100 Great Science Fiction Short Short Stories. Ed. Isaac Asimov. New York: Avon, 1985.

PP/FF: An Anthology. Ed. Peter Conners. Buffalo, NY: Starcherone, 2006.

The Pearl Jacket and Other Stories: Flash Fiction from Contemporary China. Ed. and trans. Shouhua Qi. Berkeley, CA: Stone Bridge, 2008.

Short Short Stories. Eds. Jack David and Jon Redfern. Canada: ECW, 1986.

Short Short Stories. Ed. William Ransom Wood. New York: Harcourt, 1951.

Short Shorts: An Anthology of the Shortest Shorts. Eds. Irving Howe and Ilana Wiener Howe. Boston: Godine, 1982.

Sudden Fiction: American Short-Short Stories. Eds. Robert Shapard and James Thomas. Layton, UT: Peregrine, 1986.

Sudden Fiction Continued: 60 New Short-Short Stories. Eds. Robert Shapard and James Thomas. New York: Norton, 1996.

Sudden Fiction International: 60 Short-Short Stories. Eds. Robert Shapard and James Thomas. New York: Norton, 1989.

Sudden Stories: The MAMMOTH Book of Miniscule Fiction. Ed. Dinty W. Moore. DuBois, PA: MAMMOTH, 2003.

What If? Writing Exercises for Fiction Writers, 3rd ed. Eds. Anne Bernays and Pamela Painter. New York: Longman, 2009; the short short story examples.

Word of Mouth: 150 Short-Short Stories by 90 Women Writers. Ed. Irene Zahava. Freedom, CA: Crossing, 1990.

You Have Time for This: Contemporary American Short-Short Stories. Eds. Mark Budman and Tom Hazuka. Portland, OR: Ooligan, 2007.

STORY COLLECTIONS

Atwood, Margaret. *Murder in the Dark: Short Fictions and Prose Poems*. Canada: McClelland, 1999.

Barnes, Rusty. *Breaking it Down*. Buffalo, NY: Sunnyoutside, 2007.

Brown, Randall. *Mad to Live*. Chico, CA: Flume, 2008.

Butler, Robert Olen. *Intercourse*. San Francisco: Chronicle, 2008.

Butler, Robert Olen. *Severance*. San Francisco: Chronicle, 2006.

Buzzati, Dino. *Restless Nights: Selected Stories of Dino Buzzati*. Trans. Lawrence Venuti. San Francisco: North Point, 1983.

Carlson, Ron. *A Kind of Flying*. New York: Norton, 2003.

Crace, Jim. *The Devil's Larder*. New York: Picador, 1978.

Currey, Richard. *Crossing Over: The Vietnam Stories*. Livingston, MT: Clark City, 1993.

Chinquee, Kim. *OH BABY: Flash Fiction & Prose Poetry*. Spokane, WA: Ravenna, 2008.

Clark, Amy L., Elizabeth Ellen, Kathy Fish, and Claudia Smith. *A Peculiar Feeling of Restlessness: Four Chapbooks of Short Short Fiction by Four Women*. Boston: Rose Metal, 2008.

Dybek, Stuart. *The Coast of Chicago: Stories*. New York: Knopf, 1990.

Ehrhardt, Pia Z. *Famous Father & Other Stories*. San Francisco: MacAdam/Cage, 2007.

Flick, Sherrie. *I Call This Flirting: Stories*. Chico, CA: Flume, 2004.

Forsyth, Geoffrey. *In the Land of the Free*. Boston: Rose Metal, 2008.

Galeano, Eduardo. *The Book of Embraces*. Trans. Cedric Belfrage with Mark Schafer. New York: Norton, 1992.

Helprin, Mark. *A Dove of the East: And Other Stories*. New York: Harvest/HBJ, 1990.

Hemingway, Ernest. *In Our Time*. New York: Simon, 1996.

Hempel, Amy. *The Collected Stories of Amy Hempel*. New York: Scribner, 2006.

Jaffe, Sherril. *Scars Make Your Body More Interesting & Other Stories*. Boston: Black Sparrow, 1996.

Kafka, Franz. *Franz Kafka: The Complete Stories*. Ed. Nahum N. Glatzer. New York: Schocken, 1987; the "Shorter Stories" section.

Kawabata, Yasunari. *Palm-of-the-Hand Stories*. Trans. Lane Dunlop and J. Martin Holman. New York: North Point, 1988.

Lutz, Gary. *Stories in the Worst Way*. Detroit: 3rd Bed, 2002.

Merwin, W. S. *The Miner's Pale Children*. New York: Owl, 1994.

Minot, Susan. *Lust*. New York: Vintage, 2000.

Oates, Joyce Carol. *The Assignation: Stories*. New York: HarperCollins, 1989.

Orner, Peter. *Esther Stories*. Boston: Houghton, 2001.

Ortega, Julio. *The Art of Reading: Stories and Poems*. San Antonio, TX: Wings, 2007.

Otto, Lon. *A Nest of Hooks*. Iowa City: U of Iowa P, 1978.

Painter, Pamela. *The Long and Short of It*. Pittsburgh: Carnegie-Mellon UP, 1999.

Phillips, Jayne Anne. *Black Tickets*. New York: Delta, 1979.

Rilke, Rainer Maria. *The Notebooks of Malte Laurids Brigge*. Trans. M. D. Herter. New York: Norton, 1992.

Rosa, Rodrigo Rey. *Dust on Her Tongue*. Trans. Paul Bowles. San Francisco: City Lights, 2001.

Rogers, Bruce Holland. *Flaming Arrows*. Eugene, OR: IFD, 2000.

Shapard, Robert. *Motel and Other Stories*. Ridgeway, CO: Predator, 2005.

Shua, Ana María. *Quick Fix: Sudden Fiction*. Trans. Rhonda Dahl Buchanan. Buffalo, NY: White Pine, 2008.

Songling, Pu. *Strange Tales from a Chinese Studio*. Trans. and ed. John Minford. New York: Penguin, 2006.

Williams, Diane. *excitability: Selected Stories 1986–1996*. Normal, IL: Dalkey, 1998.

Yourgrau, Barry. *Wearing Dad's Head*. New York: Arcade, 1999.

STORIES

Almond, Steve. "Moscow." *New Sudden Fiction: Short-Short Stories from America and Beyond*. Eds. Robert Shapard and James Thomas. New York: Norton, 2007.

Anderson, Sherwood. "Paper Pills." *Short Shorts: An Anthology of the Shortest Shorts*. Eds. Irving Howe and Ilana Wiener Howe. Boston: Godine, 1982.

Arzola, Jorge Luis. "Essential Things." *New Sudden Fiction: Short-Short Stories from America and Beyond*. Eds. Robert Shapard and James Thomas. New York: Norton, 2007.

Babel, Isaac. "My First Goose" and "Prischepa." *The Collected Stories of Isaac Babel*. Ed. Nathalie Babel, Trans. Peter Constantine. New York: Norton, 2002.

Barthelme, Donald. "Sentence." *City Life*. New York: Farrar, 1970.

Barthelme, Donald. "The School." *60 Stories*. New York: Penguin, 1993.

Bell, Madison Smartt. "The Naked Lady." *Sudden Fiction (Continued): 60 New Short-Short Stories*. Eds. Robert Shapard and James Thomas. New York: Norton, 1996.

Berry, Laurie. "Mockingbird." *Micro Fiction: An Anthology of Really Short Stories*. Ed. Jerome Stern. New York: Norton, 1996.

Buter, Daphne. "He Wrote Sixteen Pencils Empty." *SmokeLong Quarterly* 8 (2005). Web.

Buzzati, Dino. "The Falling Girl." *Sudden Fiction International: 60 Short-Short Stories*. Eds. Robert Shapard and James Thomas. New York: Norton, 1989.

Cadwallader, Gary. "Out of Scale." *flashquake* 11:3 (2002). Web.

Cheever, John. "Reunion." *The Stories of John Cheever*. New York: Vintage, 2000.

Dinesen, Isak. "The Blue Jar." In "The Young Man with a Carnation." *Winter's Tales*. New York: Vintage, 1993.

Dybek, Stuart. "Lights" and "Lost." *The Coast of Chicago: Stories*. New York: Knopf, 1990.

Fish, Kathy. "Wren." *FRiGG* 5 (2004). Web.

Forché, Carolyn. "The Colonel." *Flash Fiction: 72 Very Short Stories*. Eds. James Thomas, Denise Thomas, and Tom Hazuka. New York: Norton, 1992.

Fox, Robert. "A Fable." *Sudden Fiction: American Short-Short Stories*. Eds. Robert Shapard and James Thomas. Layton, UT: Peregrine, 1986.

Giles, Molly. "Protest." *Sudden Stories: The MAMMOTH Book of Miniscule Fiction*. Ed. Dinty W. Moore. DuBois, PA: MAMMOTH, 2003.

Hannah, Barry. "That's True." *Airships*. New York: Grove, 1994.

Helprin, Mark. "Because of the Waters of the Flood" and "Ruin." *A Dove of the East: And Other Stories*. New York: Harvest/HBJ, 1990.

Hemingway, Ernest. "A Very Short Story." *In Our Time*. New York: Simon, 1996.

Kafka, Franz. "The Bucket Ride." *Franz Kafka: The Complete Stories*. Ed. Nahum N. Glatzer. New York: Schocken: 1987.

Kawabata, Yasunari. "The Grasshopper and the Bell Cricket" and "The Silverberry Thief." *Palm-of-the-Hand Stories*. Trans. Lane Dunlop and J. Martin Holman. New York: North Point, 1988.

Keret, Etgar. "Asthma." *Girl on the Fridge: Stories*. New York: Farrar, 2008.

Kincaid, Jamaica. "Girl." *The Scribner Anthology of Contemporary Short Fiction: 50 North American Stories Since 1970*, 2nd ed. Eds. Michael Martone and Lex Williford. New York: Touchstone, 2007.

Knauer, Nance. "Drinking from the Well." *INK POT: Hot Pot* (Jan. 2006). Web.

Lanzarotta, Molly. "One Day Walk Through the Front Door." *What If? Writing Exercises for Fiction Writers*, 2nd ed. Eds. Anne Bernays and Pamela Painter. New York: HarperCollins, 2004.

Lisicky, Paul. "Snapshot, Harvey Cedars: 1948." *Flash Fiction: 72 Very Short Stories*. Eds. James Thomas, Denise Thomas, and Tom Hazuka. New York: Norton, 1992.

Macourek, Milos. "Jacob's Chicken." *Sudden Fiction (Continued): 60 New Short-Short Stories*. Eds. Robert Shapard and James Thomas. New York: Norton, 1996.

Martone, Michael. "Blue Hair." *Sudden Fiction (Continued): 60 New Short-Short Stories*. Eds. Robert Shapard and James Thomas. New York: Norton, 1996.

Moody, Rick. "Boys." *The Scribner Anthology of Contemporary Short Fiction: 50 North American Stories Since 1970*, 2nd ed. Eds. Michael Martone and Lex Williford. New York: Touchstone, 2007.

Monterroso, Augusto. "El Dinosaurio." *BBC News* (9 Feb., 2003). Web.

Morris, Mary. "The Haircut." *Flash Fiction: 72 Very Short Stories*. Eds. James Thomas, Denise Thomas, and Tom Hazuka. New York: Norton, 1992.

O'Brien, Tim. "Stockings." *Flash Fiction: 72 Very Short Stories*. Eds. James Thomas, Denise Thomas, and Tom Hazuka. New York: Norton, 1992.

Painter, Pamela. "Not a Ghost Story." *Vestal Review* 23 (2005). Web.

Painter, Pamela. "The New Year." *The Long and Short of It*. Pittsburgh: Carnegie-Mellon UP, 1999.

Paz, Octavio. "The Blue Boquet." *Short Shorts: An Anthology of the Shortest Stories*. Eds. Irving Howe and Ilana Wiener Howe. New York: Bantam, 1982.

Phillips, Jayne Anne. "Stars." *Black Tickets*. New York: Delta, 1979.

Pietrzyk, Leslie. "Pompeii." *New Sudden Fiction: Short-Short Stories from America and Beyond*. Eds. Robert Shapard and James Thomas. New York: Norton, 2007.

Rogers, Bruce Holland. "Three Soldiers." *You Have Time for This: Contemporary American Short-Short Stories*. Eds. Mark Budman and Tom Hazuka. Portland, OR: Ooligan, 2007.

Saunders, Tom. "Outer Space." *SmokeLong Quarterly* 10 (2005). Web.

Shapard, Robert. "Bare Ana." *Motel and Other Stories*. Ridgeway, CO: Predator, 2005.

Smith, Claudia. "My Lawrence." *New Sudden Fiction: Short-Short Stories from America and Beyond*. Eds. Robert Shapard and James Thomas. New York: Norton, 2007.

Strindberg, August. "Half a Sheet of Paper." *Short Short Stories*. Ed. William Ransom Wood. New York: Harcourt, 1951.

Sund, Robert. "Bunch Grass #37." *Bunch Grass*, 2nd ed. Seattle, WA: U of Washington P, 1973.

Udall, Brady. "The Wig." *Letting Loose the Hounds*. New York: Washington Square, 1998.

Wallace, David Foster. "Everything Is Green." *Girl with Curious Hair*. New York: Norton, 1996.

Wallace, Ron. "Worry." *Micro Fiction: An Anthology of Really Short Stories*. Ed. Jerome Stern. New York: Norton, 1996.

Wolff, Tobias. "Bullet in the Brain." *The Night in Question: Stories*. New York: Vintage, 1997.

CREDITS

ABOUT THE EDITOR

Tara L. Masih received a BA in English and a minor in sociology from C. W. Post College at Long Island University, and an MA in Writing and Publishing from Emerson College (where she taught freshman composition and grammar). As an in-house editor, she worked for Little, Brown's college division and Bedford Books of St. Martin's Press, and now freelances for companies such as Ballantine Books and Harvard University Press. Her fiction writing has won awards, and her flash has been anthologized in *Brevity & Echo* and *Word of Mouth: 150 Short-Short Stories by 90 Women Writers*. Two flash fiction chapbooks (*Fragile Skins* and *Tall Grasses*) were published by The Feral Press in 2006 and feature photographs by Joan Digby. She was a regular contributor to *The Indian-American* and *Masala* magazines, in which her essays on the topic of race and culture were often featured. Her website is www.taramasih.com.

ACKNOWLEDGMENTS

In addition to the sources fully cited in the Introduction, the following sources were referenced:

Baker, Ernest A. *The History of the English Novel: The Age of Dickens and Thackeray.* 1936. NY: Barnes, 1968.

Berne, Rebecca. "American History Through Literature, 1820–1870." Eds. Janet Gabler-Hover and Robert Sattelmeyer. Vol. 3. Detroit: Scribner's, 2006. 1077.

Cahill, Susan, ed. *Women and Fiction.* New York: Signet, 1975. xi–xix, 1–2.

Douglas, Ann. *Terrible Honesty: Mongrel Manhattan in the 1920s.* New York: Farrar, 1995.

"Encyclopedia: Yasunari Kawabata." *NationMaster.* Rapid Intelligence, n.d. Web. 9 Sept. 2008.

Fleming, Robert E. "In Our Time." *The Literary Encyclopedia.* The Literary Dictionary Co. Ltd., 17 March 2001. Web. 5 Sept. 2008.

"The Floating World of Ukiyo-e" (Library of Congress), n.d. Web. 22 June 2008.

Gwynn, R. S., ed. *Fiction,* 6th ed. New York: Pearson, 2008. 3–4.

Haugen, Hayley Mitchell, ed. *Readings on the Short Stories of Edgar Allan Poe.* The Greenhaven Press Literary Companion to American Literature. Bonnie Szumski, series ed. San Diego: Greenhaven, 2001. 12–13.

Irving, Washington. *The Sketch Book.* Cornwall, NY: Dodd, 1954.

Le Marquand, Jane. "Kate Chopin as Feminist." *Deep South* 2.3 (Spring 1996): 1. Web. 13 October 2008.

"Liberty Magazine." *RetroGalaxy.* RetroGalaxy.com, n.d. Web. 24 June, 2008.

"Rabindranath Tagore." *Wikipedia.* Wikimedia, n.d. Web. 15 August 2008.

Sawyer, Ruth. *The Way of the Storyteller.* New York: Penguin, 1976.

Stevick, Philip, ed. *The American Short Story, 1900–1945: A Critical History.* Boston: Twayne, 1984.

First, I must thank my publishers, Abby Beckel and Kathy Rooney. Not just for taking on this project and doing it justice, but for their editorial help in honing the Introduction to its present shape. Thanks also to Rebecca Saraceno for her stunning cover design, and to Crystal Pernell for her marketing assistance.

Of course this book could not exist without the contributors—I thank all for their enthusiasm, their willingness to share philosophies and teaching tips, and especially for giving up some of their own precious writing time to create these important essays. To Robbie Shapard, who helped out in myriad ways. Thanks to the family—my parents for their support; my son, Arun, for his willingness to let me work when necessary; and especially my husband, Mike Gilligan, for listening to every detail of this year-long project. To my dear writing friend, poet Mary Slechta, who keeps me connected and provides massive advice and support.

To the folks who were instrumental in helping me obtain the books and research needed for the Introduction: Toni Annable at T-Bell's Books; the family of Robert Oberfirst; St. Louis Public Library; Jean Lenville, Widener Library, Harvard; Geoff Carens and George Clark, Research Services, Lamont Library, Harvard; Rhode Island University Library; Karen Dixon, Hopkinton Town Library; Andover's Memorial Hall Library (MHL), Reference and ILL. Thanks go to everyone, but primarily to Leslie Baskin at MHL. She was able to track down the most obscure references and rare books that were crucial to completing this history. I could not have done this without her.

But most of all, to the late A. B. Guthrie, Jr.—his *Field Guide to Writing Fiction* was the inspiration for the title and initial format of this *Field Guide*—and to poet Alan King, whose comment to me on my flash writing sparked the idea for this entire endeavor—to both, a hearty thanks.

A NOTE ABOUT THE TYPE

The main text of this book is set in Robert Slimbach's Utopia. Released in 1989, Utopia was one of the first original digital text families introduced to the Adobe Originals program. As book designers began to transition to using the computer for design, the demand for high-quality digital type-faces followed. Adobe released fonts from their Originals collection to meet this demand. Utopia's balanced stroke and varied character weights make it a highly legible and versatile type family. Utopia is not without touches of elegance evident in carefully crafted letterforms.

The display text throughout this book showcases Avenir. Swiss design-er Adrian Frutiger created Avenir in 1988 for the Linotype type foundry. French for "future," Avenir most resembles, and is in fact inspired by, Paul Renner's geometric sans Futura; however Frutiger softened some of the sharp edges that pervade Futura's letterforms. The result is a more organ-ic and relaxed typeface that is stylistically fresh and yet still durable.

Sprinkled throughout the text is a dingbat that comes from the Kepler Ornaments family.

—Rebecca Saraceno